AF014

MASSIMILIANO AFIERO

AXIS FORCES
14

The Axis Forces 014 - First edition May 2020 by Luca Cristini Editor for the brand Soldiershop
Cover & Art Design by soldiershop factory.   ISBN code: 978-88-93276115
Copyright © 2020 Luca Cristini Editore (BG) ITALY.   No part of this publication may be reproduced, stored in a retrieval system or transmitted by any form or by any means, electronic, recording or otherwise without the prior permission in writing from the publishers. The publisher remains to disposition of the possible having right for all the doubtful sources images or not identifies. Visit www.soldiershop.com to read more about all our books and to buy them.

The Axis Forces number 14 – May 2020

Direction and editing

Via San Giorgio, 11 – 80021 AFRAGOLA (NA) -ITALY

Managing and Chief Editor: Massimiliano Afiero

Email: maxafiero@libero.it - **Website**: www.maxafiero.it

Contributors

Tomasz Borowski, Grégory Bouysse, Stefano Canavassi, Carlos Caballero Jurado, Rene Chavez, Gary Costello, Paolo Crippa, Carlo Cucut, Antonio Guerra, John B. Köser, Lars Larsen, Christophe Leguérandais, Eduardo M. Gil Martínez, Michael D. Miller, Peter Mooney, Péter Mujzer, Ken Niewiarowicz, Erik Norling, Raphael Riccio, Marc Rikmenspoel, Samcevich Andrei, Charles Trang, Cesare Veronesi, Sergio Volpe

---

Editorial

Hi guys. This new issue of our magazine comes out in the midst of a global pandemic crisis. This virus has caused many victims and will continue to do so if no medicines and vaccines are found to combat it as soon as possible. In every part of the world this battle is being fought against this invisible enemy and we hope that everything will be resolved as soon as possible and that we can go back to our normal life leaving this bad moment behind us. Stuck in the house, we were able to read more and dedicate ourselves to our passions and our interests, but in particular we ourselves never stopped. We continued to work, having always been teleworkers, remaining in constant contact with our collaborators all over the world. Our historical research has continued and we hope that the articles contained in this new issue of the magazine are to your liking. Of course, we always invite you to report topics and subjects that you would all like to be dealt with more in the magazine, so that we can satisfy as many readers as possible. Waiting for your comments and your reports, let's now analyze the contents of this new issue: let's start with an article dedicated to the use of the SS Totenkopf division on the Western Front in the spring of 1940. This is followed by the history of the bersaglieri (light infantry) units of the Republic Sociale Italiana, in particular of the 'Italia' division, with many unpublished photos. The biography of this issue is dedicated to one of the most important characters in the history of Waffen-SS, Paul Hausser. We continue with the second part of the article dedicated to the recruitment of the Cossacks into the German armed forces and finally we close with an interesting article dedicated to the Panzerfaust, the deadly German anti-tank weapon. Happy reading to all and see you next issue.

Massimiliano Afiero

Contents

in World War Two 1939-1945

The Totenkopf-Division
on the Western Front, Spring 1940
by Massimiliano Afiero

Theodor Eicke conferring with one of his officers, 1940.

Totenkopf **soldiers aboard a truck, May 1940.**

On May 10 1940, *Major* Stieff of the OKH operations office announced that "*...The SS-Totenkopf-Division will remain in OKH reserve in the area northwest of Cologne during the night of May 12-13*". The *Totenkopf* thus began to leave the Korbach area during the evening of May 12. Its columns crossed through Cologne and soon after turned towards the Belgian border towards Neukirchen and Wipperfürth. The division spent another four days waiting for new march orders, while most of its units were dispersed in the countryside. During this forced pause, in order to try to ease the tension of his men, Eicke organized training sessions to keep the troops busy. On the afternoon of May 17, the long-awaited march orders arrived. The duty officers thus issued orders to the various units: "*...The SS-Totenkopf-Division must put itself at the disposition of Heeresgruppe B...*".

The next day, the division was divided into several march groups. The units began their march to the west. From Neukirchen, the units moved to the west, first reaching Roermund in Holland and from there turned to the south, towards Maastricht, continuing to march to the southwest towards Dinant. During their advance across Holland and Belgium, the *Totenkopf* columns encountered no enemy resistance, as the forces under von Bock had already pushed the Allied armies back much further to the west.

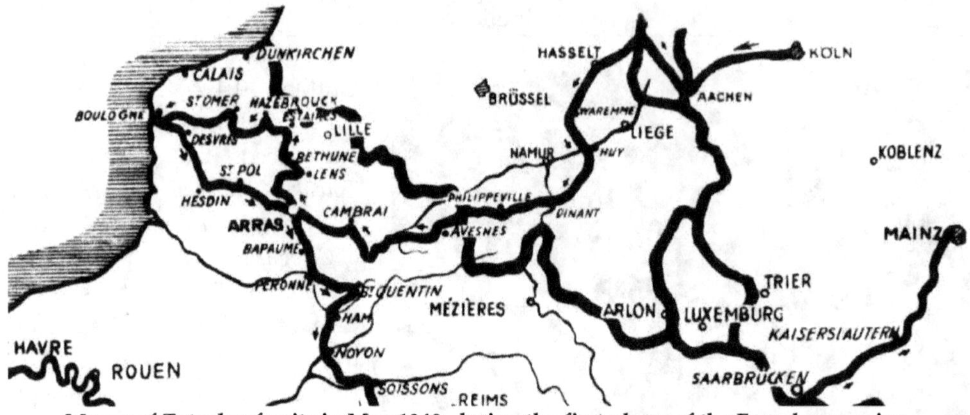

Moves of *Totenkopf* units in May 1940, during the first phase of the French campaign.

A motorized column of the *Totenkopf* on the move.

The only real obstacle to the advance were the roads crowded with military columns and fleeing civilians and in that chaos the forward elements of the division lost contact with the rest of the units.

At 21:00, the *Gen.Kdo.XV.AK* (Hoth) issued the following order: *"...The SS-Totenkopf-Division is attached to XV.AK and must move to the area Silenrieux, Barbencon, Solore, St. Géry, Grandieu, Sivry-Montbliant, Rance, Froid Chapelle, Cerfontaine"*.

On May 19, *Heeresgruppe A* had been ordered to reach the Arras sector with its mobile divisions and resume the offensive to the north and west. The *Totenkopf* left Huy and crossed the Meuse at Godine, Yvoir and Dinant. Once it reached Fraire, the division was attached to *XV.Armee-Korps*. The *Totenkopf*

Totenkopf **motorcyclists near an anti-tank ditch.**

columns drove along the same roads used by the reserve units of *Heersgruppe B*, creating many bottlenecks and delaying the advance of the troops.

A motorized column of the *Totenkopf* division under French artillery fire, May 1940.

Totenkopf motorcyclists in a Frech village, May 1940.

With the 7.Panzer-Division

Meanwhile, an order arrived to prepare to counter an enemy counterattack: Rommel's *7.Panzer-Division* had been stalled between Le Cateau and Cambrai and forced to face a violent counterattack made by French forces, with the aim of re-establishing contact with friendly forces fighting south of the Sambre River. The units of *SS-Tot.Inf.Rgt.1* were thus attached to the *7.Panzer-Division* in the area east of Maroilles (*I./SS-T.Inf.Rgt.1*) and Le Favril (*II. and III./SS-T.Inf.Rgt.1*). *SS-Staf.* Max Simon was ordered to clean out the enemy forces from the area of Mazinghein-St.Martin-Escaufourt-St. Benin. *SS-Tot.Inf.Rgt.1* under *SS-Stubaf.* Becker took the lead and crossed the Franco-Belgian border west of Grandieu, then moved on towards its objective, crossing through Avesnes, St. Hilaire and Dompierre. *II./SS-Tot.Inf.Rgt.1* under *SS-Stubaf.* Bestmann marched further to the south, passing through the localities of Clairfayts, Felleries, Marbaix and Grand-Fayt.

Totenkopf soldiers arrive in a village aboard trucks.

Totenkopf soldiers working their way through a street.

A 37 mm anti-tank gun in action, May 1940.

Around 17:00, *I./SS-Tot.Inf.Rgt.1* reached Bazuel, three kilometers east of Le Cateau. From the testimony of several prisoners, it was learned that the position at Catillon, on the Sambre Canal, was strongly defended. Max Simon set up his command post at Bazuel and quickly threw his regiment into an attack: *I./SS-Tot.Inf.Rgt.1* was to capture Catillon, while *II./SS-Tot.Inf.Rgt.1* was to take Arbre-de-Guise and St.Souplet. *III/SS-Tot.Inf.Rgt.1* was to secure the sector between Ribeauville and le Château de Colondres to block any attacks coming from the south and to head off any French troops that tried to escape from Catillon. The *2./SS-Tot.Inf.Rgt.1*, commanded by *SS-Hstuf.* Lönholdt, was positioned in the center of the attack front. It was not easy for the SS units to approach the location, as French troops had dug themselves in well, taking advantage of the thick undergrowth. After a somewhat slow advance, the SS troops finally reached Catillon, where furious house-to-house fighting flared up. Lönholdt's company finally reached the market square, after horrific hand-to-hand combat. In the meantime, *1.* and *3./SS-TIR.1* had invested the position, approaching along the canal. The *4.(MG)Kp./SS-TIR.1* had taken up positions around the village in order to block all of its exits.

in World War Two 1939-1945

A *Totenkopf* soldier on a knocked out enemy tank.

***Totenkopf* troops entering a French city, May 1940.**

The French troops, consisting mainly of Moroccan soldiers, finally became discouraged and their resistance ceased after 22:00. During the encounter the French lost 250 men. The SS also captured 55 officers as well as 1,247 NCOs and soldiers. The conquest of Chatillon was the first real military success of Theodor Eicke's division. At the same time, *II./SS-Tot.Inf.Rgt.1* attacked the position at Mazinghien. There, the French had left only a few troops as a covering force. On the other hand, the *5./Kp./SS-Tot.Inf.Rgt.1* under *SS-Hstuf.* Haussler and the *7./Kp.SS-Tot.Inf.Rgt.1* under *SS-Ostuf.* Kuntze ran into stiff resistance in front of the village of Arbre-de-Guise. As had happened at Catillon, the SS troops had to engage in hand-to-hand fighting to eliminate all of the enemy defensive positions, with the fighting lasting almost two hours. Employment of the anti-tank guns of *14.Kp./SS-Tot.Inf.Rgt.1* was decisive. Thanks to them, it was possible to wipe out the main French strongpoints. Thirteen guns and many tracked tractors were captured. From the air, the *Luftwaffe,* unaware that the town had already been taken from the enemy forces, began to bomb it; the men of *7./Kp./SS-Tot.Inf.Rgt.1* who had gathered in the cemetery were hard hit. The *6.Kp./SS-Tot.Inf.Rgt.1* led by *SS-Hstuf.* Frank had an easier job to take the village of St.Souplet, where a total of 160 enemy vehicles were captured. Near Ribeauville and St.Martin, several franc tireurs who had been left behind were swiftly eliminated. Meanwhile, *III./SS-Tot.Inf.Rgt.1* had taken up positions between Ribeauville and Château de Colondres. Several attacks made by Moroccan units of the French army were thrown back by the *9./Kp./SS-Tot.Inf.Rgt.1* led by *SS-Ostuf.* Rosenbusch.

Totenkopf troops in a French city, May 1940.

A *Pak* being towed by an half-track.

A *Pak 36* during the fighting in France, May 1940.

The *11./SS-Tot.Inf.Rgt.1* under *SS-Hstuf.* Krauth was subsequently thrown into a counterattack which enabled to Moroccans to be rooted from their positions. About a hundred prisoners were taken as a result of the engagement. During its first day of combat, the *Totenkopf* division suffered fifteen dead and forty-eight wounded.

The battle for Arras

On May 20, 1940, *Totenkopf* was ordered to reach the Sambre River with two regimental groups, which were to get as far as Cambrai and continue on to Saint Pol, south of Arras. It was transferred to the subordination of *XXXIX.Armee-Korps* under General Rudolf Schmidt, taking up positions between *8.Pz.Div.* to the south and *7.Pz.Div.* to the north. Around noon, the regimental group of *SS-Tot.Inf.Rgt.3* reached the eastern suburbs of Cambrai, passing through Avesnes, Landrecies and Le Cateau; *I./SS-Tot.Inf.Rgt.3* crossed through the city and took up positions on the heights at Rallencourt. Cambrai had suffered a bombing three days earlier and its populace had joined the columns fleeing along the French roads. The *II.* and *III./SS-Tot.Inf.Rgt.3* assumed positions north and northwest of Cambrai.

An SS anti-tank crew emplacing its gun, May 1940.

A French tank hit and in flames in the Arras sector.

Some British troops tried to break into the city. The British soldiers, in order to trick the Germans, used a ruse that was contrary to the rules of war: exiting from an armored car, some soldiers dressed in German uniforms opened fire on a group from *II./SS-Tot.Inf.Rgt.3*. This incident was reported in the march journal of the division's medical officer and was a determining factor in the behavior of the SS soldiers in the following days. At 14:00, the division headquarters left Sivry and set itself up in Niergnies. On 21 May, at 1:10, *SS-Tot.Inf.Rgt.3* assumed a covering position for *7.Pz.Div.* south of Arras, with *I./SS-Tot.Inf.Rgt.3* of *SS-Stubaf.* Bellwidt at Wailly, *II./SS-Tot.Inf.Rgt.3* under *SS-Stubaf.* Petersen at Mercatel and *III./SS-Tot.Inf.Rgt.3* under *SS-Stubaf.* Dusenschön at Neuville-Vitasse.

PzKpfw 35(t) tanks on the Western Front, May 1940.

Totenkopf troops in France.

A damaged *PzKpfw 35(t)* of *Totenkopf*, May 1940.

A battery of *Totenkopf* howitzers in action, May 1940.

During the morning, after more than a day of hesitation, Hitler decided to send von Rundstedt's armored forces to the north to wipe out the trapped Allied units. In accordance with that decision, at 14:00 Eicke received the order to cross the River Scarpe in force. *SS-Tot.Inf.Rgt.3* accordingly began to march at 14:30, with the support of *I./SS-T.Art.Rgt.* and elements of *SS-T.Aufkl.-Abt.* At practically the same moment, the British 5th and 50th infantry divisions, supported by the 1st Armoured Brigade, launched a counterattack from Tilloy, Achicourt and Dainville to try to open a corridor to the south towards the 1st Army Group of General Billotte. Around 15:00, on the hills of Simencourt, two British tanks broke into the *7.Pz.Div.* rear area and attacked the columns of *I./SS-Tot.Inf.Rgt.3*, in particular those of

4.Kompanie, that were moving to the north. Two trucks were destroyed and the company suffered its first three dead. The companies that had not been touched continued their march towards Wanquetin. A warning message arrived from the headquarters of *XXXIX.Armee-Korps* for the *Totenkopf*: "*...Major enemy attack south of Bapaume*".

A British *Matilda* tank destroyed by *Totenkopf* troops, May 1940.

A *Totenkopf Pak 35/36* on the side of a road, May 1940.

Around 15:10, six *Matilda* tanks overran *Pz.Jg.Abt.42*, whose 37 mm *Pak 36* guns proved incapable of penetrating the armor of the British tanks. Panic seized the men of *7.Pz.Div.*, who were impotent in the face of the enemy tank attack. The British continued their advance towards the Ficheux-Mercatel road, while another unit attacked Ficheux, moving from Agny. In the meantime, *SS-Tot.Inf.Rgt.3*, coming from Mercatel, closed in on Ficheux, parallel to the railway line. The *5.Kp/SS-Tot.Inf.Rgt.3* found itself facing the British tanks. Numerous trucks were hit and caught fire. *SS-Ustuf.* Barnickel's platoon took cover while some of the men hid in the cellars of several houses. Some trucks continued on towards Ficheux to escape from the enemy tanks. Six *PzKpfw 35(t)* of *3.(s)Kp./SS-T.Aufkl.-Abt.* went into action near the crossroads east of Mercatel, managing to free the men of *Nachrichten-Abteilung 83* of *7.Panzer-Division*. At the same time, while some of the units of *SS-Tot.Inf.Rgt.3* were reaching Lattre St.Quentin around 16:00, *III./SS-Tot.Inf.Rgt.3* was attacked west of Mercatel by many enemy tanks. The *14.(Pz.Abw.)Kp./SS-Tot.Inf.Rgt.3* was called to reinforce; *SS-Ustuf.* Ernst Wagner's platoon, with its 37 mm *Pak 36* guns, took up positons on both sides of the railway line. To the west of Mercatel, *2.Bttr.SS-T.Art.Rgt.* fired over open sights with its 105 mm howitzers against the British tanks.

British *Matilda* tanks that have been hit in the woods.

***Totenkopf* signals personnel.**

A *Waffen-SS* anti-tank gun in its firing position.

Positioned on a small hill situated to the west of the railway line was the *Pak* of *SS-Unterscharführer* Elsner: *"…We were the first to arrive on the hill. There was not enough time to dig into the ground to emplace our guns. As soon as we got our gun into battery, the first tanks appeared on the hill facing us. I let them get to within eight hundred meters before giving the order 'Fire at will!'. The first round fell too short. The second passed to the right of the tank. But, the third hit the target. A second tank met the same fate at six hundred meters. Our company commander, SS-Hstuf. Pfeiffer, also joined in and hit a third tank. Machine gun fire coming from our right and our front hit our positions. We therefore had to shift a hundred meters to the right… From our new position, we spotted many enemy tanks coming towards us. Another two tanks were knocked out, but the machine gun fire became even more intense…".* The British were able to take the railway embankment. The SS units had managed to destroy numerous light tanks, but were completely impotent against the heavy tanks. The men were seized by panic and suffered heavy losses. Two *PzKpfw. 35(t)* of the recon group were destroyed during the fighting.

A *Totenkopf* machine gun team with an *MG-34*.

A *Totenkopf* truck column through a French village.

Their crews saved themselves but suffered more or less serious burns. Further to the west, *3.Kp./SS-T.Pz.Abw.-Abt.* was also engaged against other British tanks. Its nine *Pak* guns took positions around Ficheux. An SPW broke into the area. An officer came up and asked *SS-Rttf.* Semmler of the logistics train of *3.Kp./SS-T.Inf.Rgt.3* where the headquarters was of the *SS-Totenkopf-Division*. The SS corporal replied with a downward movement of his finger. Furious over the unmilitary gesture, the officer jumped from his armored vehicle and shouted at the SS soldier : *"Soldier, don't you know who I am?"*. It was none other than General Rommel, commander of *7.Pz.Div.*, trying to find his *Schützen-Regiment 7*. Meanwhile the battle had intensified. The 37 mm rounds were ineffective against the thick armor of the Matildas, so the SS gunners began to fire at the tracks and were able to stop eight enemy tanks. These successes were possible due to the slowness of the British tanks. With respect to the enemy infantry, it was fended off by *II./SS-T.Inf.Rgt.3*. Near the crossroads of Bac-du-Nord at Rivière, the British tanks were repulsed by *I./SS-T.Inf.Rgt.3*, supported by *1.Bttr./SS-T.Art.Rgt.*; one tank was knocked out and another immobilized. Despite their heavy losses, the British and French did not give up the fight. To the east of Brétencourt, the British tanks advance parallel to the road to Blairville. They reached Hendcourt and threatened the flank of *SS-Tot.Inf.Rgt.2*, whose positions ran along the Wancourt-St.Martin-Hénin-Boisleux road.

SS-Stubaf. **Sander in the center, wearing motorcyclists goggles, with other officers.**

Totenkopf **soldiers going into an attack, May 1940.**

I./SS-Tot.Inf.Rgt.2 under *SS-Stubaf.* Fortenbacher reached Ransart just as the first British tanks arrived. The *3.Kp/SS-Tot.Inf.Rgt.2* led by *SS-Hstuf.* Knöchelein quickly established positions in the cemetery area. The situation was identical to that of *II./SS-T.Inf.Rgt.2* engaged against British units with two platoons of *13.(IG)Kp./SS-Tot.Inf.Rgt.2*. Most of the regiment continued to advance on Beaumetz. After a sharp engagement, some enemy tanks were pushed back north of the town, at the cost of high losses; the anti-tank platoon alone suffered three *Pak* destroyed and seven men killed. A fresh tank attack, this time by French *Hotchkiss* tanks, involved the front held by *III./SS-Tot.Inf.Rgt.2* led by *SS-Stubaf.* Schleifenbaum, along the Croisilles-Rivière-Beaumetz road. Their breakthrough created great confusion among the SS ranks. Panic seized the truck drivers who began to flee.

Totenkopf **soldiers fighting in a French village, May 1940.**

French tanks knocked out and abandoned by their crews.

III./SS-T.Art.Rgt., which had arrived in the area, also ended up under French fire. *SS-Stubaf.* Sander's vehicle was hit. His driver was killed. Sander and his aide, *SS-Ustuf.* Dauselt, took refuge in a ditch. The SS units tried to reorganize themselves as quickly as possible in order to avoid a disastrous rout. *SS-Stubaf.* Heinz Lammerding, advancing along the road to Aubigny with his engineer battalion, then took the initiative, assuming command of all the units that were in the area, with the objective of clearing out Simencourt. *SS-Stubaf.* Lammerding stopped the infantry units that had panicked and sent the *2.Kp./SS-T.Pi.Btl.* to Beaumetz along with a battery of *III./SS-Tot.Art.Rgt.* The SS engineers defended the artillery gun emplacements, surrounding them with minefields. In addition, some howitzers were emplaced in battery along with the *Pak* of *14.(Pz.Abw.)Kp./SS-Tot.Inf.Rgt.2*, while the men of *9.Kp./SS-Tot.Inf.Rgt.2* arrived as reinforcements. *SS-Ustuf.* Dörner of *2.Kp./SS-T.Pi.Btl.* led a scouting patrol towards Simencourt, where elements of *9.Kp./SS-Tot.Inf.Rgt.2* were clashing with enemy tanks. The engineers of *2.Kp./SS-T.Pi.Btl.* then attacked the enemy tanks that had broken into the area, at close range, with magnetic mines, risking their own lives.

France, May 1940: a column of half-tracks towing anti-tank guns, on the move.

Advance into enemy territory, May 1940.

Around 16:00, British tanks arrived in the area west of Mercatel, crossed by *III./SS-Tot.Inf.Rgt.3* coming from Neuville-Vitasse. Some vehicles were hit and immediately caught fire. The SS jumped from their trucks seeking cover, fleeing from Mercatel. A total rout was avoided thanks to the intervention of some 88 mm guns from *2.Bttr./Flak-Abt.86* that knocked out a number of British tanks. Around 18:00, the *Stukas* appeared in the sky and put a definitive halt to the Allied counterattack. It was a terrible day for the *Totenkopf*, as some of its units had shown signs of panic, especially those of the logistics train. Its losses had been high: 39 killed, 66 wounded and two missing. In addition, the Allied counterattack forced Theodor Eicke to temporarily suspend his attack towards the north at Valhoun.

Totenkopf **engineers at work.**

A *Totenkopf* truck crossing a brigde, May 1940.

This had been mounted by *I./SS-Tot.Inf.Rgt.3* via Wanquetin, Habarcq and Hermaville, towards the River Scarpe, at Aubigny. Around 19:00, *SS-Stubaf.* Bellwidt's battalion reached Aubigny, still being defended by groups of Allied soldiers. It was reached by *SS-Tot.Inf.Rgt.1* during the night, which had to clear out the village. The following day, Theodor Eicke set up his headquarters there. According to the march journal of *SS-Obf.* von Montigny, several Allied tanks accompanied by infantry tried to withdraw to the south, passing through the streets of Aubigny. The situation became very confused. The *Luftwaffe* dropped some bombs from on high, creating even more confusion. *SS-Tot.Inf.Rgt.1* registered its first losses. French franc tireurs, in civilian clothes fired on the SS soldiers, among other things employing "dum-dum" bullets. These snipers were in reality French soldiers who had been cut off following the rapid German advance. In reprisal, about a hundred French civilians were killed by SS units, by order of Eicke himself. That same day, another reprisal took place; a unit of *SS-Tot.Inf.Rgt.2* that was marching along the road of Saint-Pol-sur-Ternoise stopped in the village of Berles-Monchel, near Vandelicourt, apparently searching for British soldiers, and was interrogating civilians. Some of the civilians, terrorized by the appearance of the German soldiers, began to flee. At that point the SS soldiers, possibly fearing a possible ambush, began to throw grenades and fire on the civilians who were attempting to flee. Other civilians were also soon shot. At the end of the sweep, forty-five French civilian victims were dead. The day ended with an attack by *SS-Tot.Inf.Rgt.1* against the hills at Hallicourt and another by *SS-Tot.Inf.Rgt.3* towards Cloques. Meanwhile, *SS-Tot.Inf.Rgt.2* continued its advance towards Béthune.

Theodor Eicke, with binoculars, following the progress of the battle.

SS scouts checking a map, May 1940.

On the La Bassée Canal

On May 23, the division was attached to *XIV.Armee-Korps* of General Hoepner, to support it in its offensive towards the La Bassée canal, with the mission of preventing the British from digging in along that natural defensive line. At that moment, the situation was very confused in that area. To that end, *3.(s)Kp./SS-T.Aufkl.-Abt.* was engaged in several recon missions around Vendin and Béthune, to intercept any enemy units. The British had erected barriers to the entrances of the two villages, which were removed by the SS scouts. Meanwhile, *SS-Tot.Inf.Rgt.1* continued its advance to the northeast, reaching the hills situated to the east of Hallicourt. The division's left flank was covered by *SS-*

Tot.Inf.Rgt.3 at Bruay and Division. At Choques, *3.Kp./SS-Tot.Inf.Rgt.3* captured a train that had twenty-eight French tanks and field hospital aboard. Six *Hotchkiss H-39* tanks were repainted with German colors and markings and integrated into the *3.(s)Kp./SS-T.Aufkl.-Abt.* to replace the *Pz.Kpfw.35(t)* tanks that had been destroyed two days earlier. The *SS-Tot.Inf.Rgt.2* units were kept in reserve in the Marles les Mines-Houdain sector, and their mere presence served to terrorize the French civilian population.

A French *Somua 35* tank captured and re-used by the *Totenkopf.* An SS artillery observer.

Totenkopf and *Luftwaffe* soldiers observing the devastating effect of an 88mm *Flak* gun against enemy tanks on the French front, May 1940.

While the SS troops were engaged in searching frantically for a crossing point over the canal, other British units, mainly infantry, who were retreating to the north arrived to reinforce the positions facing the *Totenkopf.* On May 24, around noon, *SS-Tot.Inf.Rgt.1* was ordered to cross the La Bassée canal at Béthune and Beuvry and to establish bridgeheads at the same time. *SS-Tot.Inf.Rgt.1* was engaged on the left, to the east of Béthune. The objective of *III./SS-Tot.inf.Rgt.1* was the sector of the canal at Beuvry. The right flank was covered by *II./SS-Tot.Inf.Rgt.1*, whose command was assigned to *SS-Hstuf.* Lönholdt following the wounding of *SS-Stubaf.* Deisenhofer. The *1.Kp./SS-T.Pi.-Btl.* under *SS-Ostuf.* Siegfried Müller and *II./SS-T.Art.Rgt.* of *SS-Stubaf.* Priess, were charged with supporting the infantry attack. The SS artillerymen emplaced their guns, enlisting the assistance of several French civilians. British resistance proved to be very strong and the canal was not reached until around 17:00 at the cost of heavy losses. At Beuvry, near the bridge at Gorre, the deafening sounds of battle were replaced by total silence. A *Totenkopf* motorcyclist headed towards the bridge without realizing that it had been destroyed.

SS motorcyclists remove an obstruction from the entrance to the village.

A *Totenkopf* sidecar on the move. On the ground, helmets and rifles left by fleeing enemy, May 1940.

Not able to stop in time, he ended up in the canal with his motorcycle. The five sidecar motorcycles that were following him fortunately were able to stop in time, after which their crews dismounted, only to be taken quickly under fire by a *Panhard* armored car. The bulk of *III./SS-Tot.Inf.Rgt.1* then entered the neighborhood of Quesnoy, occupying the houses along the canal after having attacked them and cleared them out with hand grenades. On the northern bank, the British had in the meantime reinforced significantly with troops from the 2nd, 44th and 48th infantry divisions. All of the bridges had been destroyed by enemy forces and crossing the canal now seemed impossible. Nevertheless, the SS troops made it to the opposite bank using rubber rafts provided by the engineers, even managing to bring across several anti-tank guns and other heavy weapons.

Totenkopf soldiers watching a barge pass by along a canal, May 1940.

An SS artillery rangefinder.

During the attacks that followed, the SS troops were able to overrun positions defended by elements of the Queen's Own Cameron Highlanders, thus establishing an initial bridgehead on the northern bank of the canal. The heavy weapons were emplaced straightaway to prepare for new attacks and at the same time to defend against any enemy counterattacks.

The order to halt!

At that very moment, an urgent message arrived from the headquarters of *XVI.Armee-Korps*: *Totenkopf* was to immediately suspend the attack, withdraw to the southern bank of the canal and prepare to defend against an imminent enemy tank attack. The armored and motorized units of *Heeresgruppe A* were to suspend their advance and those units that were already across the canal had to withdraw. This adoption of the defensive posture was in line with Hitler's order of May 24, which called for the troops to halt along the canal and not to push towards Dunkirk. The order had been signed by the *Führer* himself, on the advice of von Rundstedt, who had proposed waiting for the arrival of other forces before attacking the enemy.

Totenkopf **soldiers making ready to cross a canal on rubber rafts.**

Totenkopf **forward artillery observers.**

In addition, preparations had to be made for an attack to the south to definitively destroy the French army. Göring also convinced Hitler that the *Luftwaffe* on its own would be enough to wipe out the great Allied pocket. In reality this pause served only to give the Allies some breathing space and to deliberately prepare the evacuation by sea of their troops from French soil to England (*Operation Dynamo*). The order infuriated Eicke: he had lost a number of men to cross the canal and now was ordered to abandon the positions that had been seized. The withdrawal, under the eyes of the enemy, would only cause further losses. In fact, when the British noted the movement in the *Totenkopf* bridgehead, they began to fire with all available weapons. Complicating the *Totenkopf* movements, fire from British artillery located north of Bethune also began to fall. Losses to the division on May 24, alone amounted to 43 killed (among which were four officers), 121 wounded and five missing! Hoepner and Eicke had an animated discussion regarding the latest fighting.

in World War Two 1939-1945

Eicke being briefed on the situation by a subordinate.

Totenkopf **troops crossing the canal, May 1940.**

Hoepner reprimanded Eicke for his lack of attention to preparing for the offensive action and the recklessness with which he had thrown his men into the attack. Hoepner also accused the SS units of having deliberately committed crimes against the civilian populace, in particular at Quesnoy: after having taken up positions along the southern bank of the canal, the men under *SS-Stubaf.* Bestmann had in fact turned numerous civilians out of their houses and had executed a total of forty-eight people. While the Germans were stalled along the southern bank of the canal, the British continued to pound the *Totenkopf* positions with mortars and artillery while further reinforcing their defensive positions. The troops of *SS-Tot.Inf.Rgt.3* had also established defensive positions along the canal in the Choques area. At Hinges, elements of *III./SS-Tot.Inf.Rgt.3* and engineers from *3.Kp./SS-T.Pi.-Btl.* were involved in new and useless reprisals against the civilian population, following several alleged attacks by enemy franc tireurs. On June 25, the *Totenkopf* units continued to remain immobile along the canal; *SS-Tot.Inf.Rgt.2* was on the left and *SS-Tot.Inf.Rgt.3* was on the right. The forward posts were situated along the line Carvin-Bois de Paquebaut-Locon-Les Choquaux. British artillery hit the SS positions throughout the day. The *Totenkopf* had been formally prohibited from crossing the canal in force and had to be satisfied with sending scouting patrols across to the opposite bank.

A *Pak 35/36* deployed along the water's edge.

A *Totenkopf* defensive position along the La Bassée Canal.

The offensive resumes

On May 26, after noontime, the order was finally given to resume the offense. The attack was launched at 19:40 by *I./SS-Tot.Inf.Rgt.3*, which crossed the canal at 20:30. At 23:30, the position of Locon was taken by SS troops. Further to the left, *I./SS-Tot.Inf.Rgt.2* crossed the canal at Pont-Sapplie (*2.Kp.*) and Pont-du-Curé (*3.Kp.*). At 22:30, *3.Kp./SS-Tot.Inf.Rgt.2* captured Riez-du-Vinage and continued on towards Le Cornet Malo before assuming the defensive north of the woods at Paqueaut. On May 27, at 3:00, the *3.(s)Kp./SS-T.Aufkl.-Abt.*, consisting of seven tanks, attacked the position at Hinges to then continue on towards Le Cornet Malo. The *II.* and *III./SS-Tot.Inf.Rgt.2* crossed the canal in turn at 4:30. British resistance was very spirited and losses were very heavy. *II./SS-Tot.Inf.Rgt.3* also went on the attack towards Le Cornet Malo. The action was not however successful, despite the support by the tanks of the reconnaissance group. The lead company, *5.Kp./SS-Tot.Inf.Rgt.3*, lost its commander, *SS-Hstuf.* Martin Lietz. A new combat group was then thrown into the assault, led by *SS-Ostuf.* Töpperwein and was able after violent close-quarter fighting to take the position at Le Cornet Malo. Further to the west, *SS-Tot.Inf.Rgt.2* attacked towards Boheme and Le Cornet Malo, moving from the area of Riez-du-Vinage. The attack was launched by *I./SS-Tot.Inf.Rgt.2*, with *3.Kp.* led by *SS-Hstuf.* Fritz Knöchlein in the center, *SS-Ostuf.* Reinhard Löw's *2.Kp.* north of the woods of

Paqueaut and *1.Kp.* under *SS-Hstuf.* Hans Kaltofen in a covering role on the left. The *4.(MG)Kp.* of *SS-Hstuf.* Schrödel was in support with its heavy machine guns. Around 6:30, the line La Boheme-Le Cornet Malo-Carvin was reached, but the SS troops suffered heavy losses because of the stiff British resistance. In addition, *SS-Staf.* Heinz Bertling had dispersed his regiment too far to the north without adequately protecting his flanks.

Totenkopf **soldiers in the streets of le Cornet Malo, May 1940.**

SS-Staf. **Götze in France, May 1940.**

As a consequence, he lost contact with the rest of the division and Theodor Eicke had to send *I./SS-Tot.Inf.Rgt.3* on the attack. The battalion, reinforced with *9.Kp.*, went on the attack at 11:30, advancing towards Zelobes. Shortly after, it was ordered to relieve *II./SS-Tot.Inf.Rgt.3* at Le Cornet Malo. He then left RN 345 to attack from the Rue du Paradis, under terrible enemy barrage fire: *SS-Staf.* Götze, who was in the midst of his men, was mortally wounded. *SS-Ostubaf.* Josias zu Erbprinz Waldeck und Prymont assumed temporary command of the regiment. On that flat terrain devoid of cover, the SS troops suffered heavy losses and their attacks were stopped cold. At 16:00, the position at Le Paradis was attacked from the west by *II./SS-Tot.Inf.Rgt.2*. Its commander, *SS-Stubaf.* Kummer, was wounded during the fighting and was replaced by the commander of *6.Kp.*,

SS-Hstuf. Dallinger. *SS-Ostuf.* Albrecht, commander of *5.Kp./SS-Tot.Inf.Rgt.2*, seized by panic, refused to lead his men and sought refuge in a hole, far from the front line.

Prisoners captured by *Totenkopf* **in the Cornet Malo sector (***Charles Trang Collection***).**

SS-Hstuf. **Fritz Knöchlein.**

A resolute platoon leader then led the attack. *I./SS-Tot.Inf.Rgt.2* also ran into serious difficulty, being stalled in an open field by enemy fire coming from the farm at de Duries. Some howitzers from *7.Bttr./SS-Tot.Art.-Rgt.* were then brought up to the front line to respond to the enemy fire. The British troops were forced to withdraw to a new defensive line along the Lawe Canal between Lestrem and Vielle Chapelle, where they were reinforced by fresh troops.

Massacre at Le Paradis

About two kilometers further west, about a hundred men of the 2nd Royal Norfolk had barricaded themselves at the *de Duries* farm, with their commander *Major* Dyer. They had been ordered to slow down the advance of the *Totenkopf* troops for as long as possible. The farmhouse was surrounded soon after by troops from *I./SS-Tot.Inf.Rgt.2*, led by *SS-Hstuf.* Fritz Knöchlein. The British soldiers put up a stiff resistance, firing with rifles and machine guns for about an hour, causing further losses to the SS troops and using, according to the Germans, *"dum-dum"* bullets. They held out until 17:15 when, with their ammunition exhausted, they decided to surrender; they raised a white flag, threw down their weapons and came out into the open with their hands raised. The prisoners were assembled near the Creton farm, where they were massacred by fire from two heavy machine guns. At the end of it all 97 victims were dead.

A *Totenkopf* column stalled by enemy fire in the Le Paradis area, May 1940.

***Totenkopf* soldiers and vehicles near a burning farmhouse.**

Those not yet dead were finished off with bayonets. Once this summary execution was over, Knöchlein gathered his men and headed towards Estaires to rejoin his regiment. Two British soldiers had, however, survived that horrific slaughter; covered by the corpses of their friends, they escaped death, being only wounded. When the SS troops left the site of the execution, these two miraculous survivors, privates Albert Pooley and William O'Callaghan, took shelter at another farm where they remained for several days, until they were captured by troops from the *251.Infanterie-Division*. Their testimony after the war was enough to indict Fritz Knöchlein, who was hanged in January 1949. When news of the massacre at Le Paradis began to spread, the commander of *XVI.Armee-Korps*, General Hoepner, immediately ordered an investigation. The news of crimes committed by the *Totenkopf* circulated for about a week and Hoepner, without any concrete proof, issued a special order threatening court martial for anyone who had executed even a single prisoner.

Moving forward again

The *Totenkopf* troops resumed their northward advance, on the heels of the Allied troops that were withdrawing towards the coast and which continued to fight doggedly. The Allied defensive line now ran along the Lys Canal between Estaires and Merville. On the evening of the 27th, Eicke's exhausted men, after having made contact with the new enemy positions, dug in for the night, limiting themselves to responding to the British fire. While his troops were halted, Eicke received new orders from Hoepner: at dawn on the 28th he was to attack Estaires in force and secure a bridgehead on the other side of the Lys Canal. The *XVI.Armee-Korps* objective consisted of forcing the new Allied defensive line, advancing northeast and cutting off the retreat of enemy forces towards Dunkirk. The *Totenkopf* was to lead the attack. The *Totenkopf* units moved to attack between Vielle Chapelle and Pont-du-Hem at 8:00 on 28 May, following preparatory artillery fire. Reconnaissance patrols had reported that the enemy occupied Vielle Chapelle in strength and that the bridge over the canal had been destroyed. The infantry was forced to cross the canal on makeshift boats, sustaining heavy losses because of enemy sniper fire. The *Totenkopf* troops reached the line Picantin-Laventie during the early afternoon hours with *SS-Tot.Inf.Rgt.1*. The SS troops quickly reached the crossroads at Rouge-Croix. British resistance intensified at Laventie. Considering the strong enemy resistance, General Hoepner counseled Eicke to shift the axis of attack to the west of Estaires, where the enemy defenses seemed to be weaker. Soon after, *Totenkopf* troops again attacked Laventie successfully, continuing on as far as Croix, pushing the British rear guards towards Lalestrem. That same afternoon, *SS-Tot.Inf.Rgt.3* was subordinated to *4.Panzer-Division* in the Richebourg-Aubers-Fromelles area. On the morning of the 29th, the *Totenkopf* again attacked in force reaching Lys and the hills at Kemel. General Hermann Hoth, Hoepner's superior as commander of the armored group, ordered Eicke to pursue the enemy forces and not to give them any pause, reminding him to cover his flanks. The enemy continued to withdraw to the north, with the German troops at their heels. On the left flank of the corps, *Totenkopf* was ordered to take Estaires. *SS-Tot.Inf.Rgt.1* entered the town late in the morning and the British fell back to the north. The SS troops took off in pursuit. At 16:00, Bailleul was captured by *SS-Tot.Inf.Rgt.2*. In the evening, *SS-Tot.Inf.Rgt.1* made contact with units of *6.Armee* (*Heeresgruppe B*) coming from the northeast, closing the ring around the Allied forces which now had their backs to the sea. However, only five French divisions were surrounded, while the bulk of the British Expeditionary Force and of the French 1st Army had been able to withdraw to Dunkirk.

Bibliography

M. Afiero, *"Totenkopf"*, Marvia Edizioni
M. Afiero, *"3.SS-Pz.Div. Totenkopf - Vol. I: 1939-1943"*, Associazione Culturale Ritterkreuz
M. Afiero, *"The 3rd Waffen-SS Pz.Div. Totenkopf 1939-1943: Vol.1"*, Schiffer Publishing
M. Afiero, *"Totenkopf I: 1939-1942"*, Almena Ediciones

Bersaglieri's Units of Italian Social Republic

by Paolo Crippa and Carlo Cucut

Poster inciting enrollment in the 1st Bersaglieri Division "*Italia*" (*Paolo Crippa collection*).

Heuberg: Group of Bersaglieri during training for interview with German instructors (*Viziano*).

The general disarray caused by the Armistice on September 8, 1943, also had immediate repercussions on the Bersaglieri's units, both present in the Peninsula and abroad. The Bersaglieri, however, were among the first to reorganize and take up arms again, both in the South, where at the end of September 1943 the LI Battalion of *Bersaglieri* was included in the First Motorized Group, and in the North. In the territory of what would later be the Italian Social Republic, the first non-politicized department to take up arms again alongside the Germanic Ally was the Bersaglieri Battalion "*Mussolini*", which began re-establishing itself in Verona on 11st September in the barracks of the 8th Bersaglieri Regiment, nucleus of what would later be the "*Luciano Manara*" Bersaglieri Regiment. In Milan, the 3rd Volunteer Regiment was formed, with personnel from the Regio Esercito Regiment of the same name, and during the following weeks four Battalions, XVIII, XX, XXV and LI were formed. At the beginning of 1944 the Regiment Command was moved to Germany to reach the "*Italia*" Bersaglieri Division in constitution and the battalions that formed it became autonomous, changing the numbering. The *"Italia"* Bersaglieri Division was established in Heuberg in Germany with volunteers from the concentration camps and was then deployed south of Parma, fought in Garfagnana and disbanded on April 28th in Val di Taro.

In the Heuberg training camp the Bersaglieri of "Italia" Division gained confidence even with German weapons, such as these machine gunners with an *MG-42* (*Viziano*).

Bersaglieri of "Italia" Division during training.

Outside the national territory we remember the events of the Bersaglieri Battalion *"Zara"*, emblematic of that terrible moment of passage, caused by September 8th. Displaced since 1941 in the area of the redeemed city, in fact isolated from the rest of the Kingdom of Italy, the Bersaglieri *Zara* Battalion had participated, together with other Italian and German unitts, in continuous containment actions. At the time of the Armistice, the Battalion, which was stationed as a garrison in the town of Biograd (Zaravechia), fell back on Zara, where the officers found themselves faced with a dilemma: to collaborate with the Germans or end up in prison camps, given that it was impossible to attempt a resistance against the Germanic armed forces. A compromise was reached: the Italians would remain as garrison of the city, to defend it above all against the reaction and the annexation ambitions of the Croatian Ustashas. The Battalion thus dedicated itself to this exhausting garrison activity, but, with a slow but inexorable haemorrhage, the city's units gradually lost men, some of them sent in Germany, others escaped among the partisans or fleeing to their homes in Venezia Giulia.

Demonstration of "*Italia*" in Heuberg in the presence of General Mainardi, commander of the Division (*Viziano*).

Demonstration of "*Italia*" division in Heuberg.

After the first terrible Allied bombing in the autumn of 1943, what remained of the battalion, about 200 men, was transferred to Trieste to become part of the army of the R.S.I. January 4th, 1944. Some Bersaglieri wanted to stay and, disarmed by the Germans, they were sent to various neighboring localities to be employed as labor-power.

1st Bersaglieri Div."Italia"

The "*Italia*" Bersaglieri Division was officially established in November 1943, but only in the spring of 1944 it begun its training in the Heuberg Camp in Pomerania. It was made up of former internees, conscripts and volunteers from the Great Unit Constitution Center.

Bersagliere in training at Heuberg (*Viziano*).

Training of the Bersaglieri of "*Italia*" Division in the use of portable radios (*Viziano*).

Completed the training period, on 17th July 1944 it marched in front of the Duce, receiving, at the end of the parade, the combat flags for its Regiments. It seemed therefore that the time of the return of "Italy" to its homeland had come but, due to the controversy that broke out with the Germans about the sending of thousands of Italian soldiers to Germany to be incorporated into the *Flak* and the withdrawal of the German armament destined for the constitutions German divisions to be sent to the western front, the Division's final training was blocked, to resume in August and ended in the fall. It was therefore only in the month of December 1944 that the Division was able to return to Italy, with a transfer made particularly difficult by the lack of means of transport and by the aerial bombardments of the railway lines which, causing multiple interruptions, forced many Units to finish the journey for railway to Brescia or Verona, and to complete the transfer on foot to the Division's concentration area, located between Parma, Sala Baganza (PR) and Pontremoli (MS). The transfers on foot were carried out during the night, to avoid air strikes, with stretches of even 50 kilometers in length, in extremely critical weather conditions, causedby heavy rain and snow. Once in the assigned area, the Divisional Command was placed in Ozzano (BO), the 1st Bersaglieri Regiment in Berceto (PR), the 2nd Bersaglieri Regiment in the North West of Collecchio (PR), east of the Taro River, the 4th Regiment Artillery between Collecchio and Ozzano, the 4th Exploring Group in Sala Baganza, the Tank Hunters in Fornovo (PR), the Services and the Intendancy in Felino (PR) and Sala Baganza. The fatigue of the transfer, the conditions of the clothing, the situation of dispersion in so many nucleuses, favored the propaganda of the civilians and of the partisans who incited to the desertion, beyond to loosen the discipline. In the early days of January 1945, the German Command began the Operation *"Totila"*, a vast anti-partisan round-up in the mountain area in the Parma area between Borgo Val di Taro, Bardi, Bedonius, and the rear of Aulla.

Front of the *"Gothic"*: the Bersaglieri of the *"Italia"* Division enter the line (*Viziano*).

Bersaglieri of *"Italia"* Division in a hole armed with a 81mm mortar (*Viziano*).

The Bersaglieri of the 2nd Regiment of the *"Italia"* Division also participated in the roundup. Towards the middle of January 1945 the transfer of the "Italia" to the line of the Serchio Valley began, through the Passo della Cisa, Pontremoli and Aulla, a transfer that was carried out especially at night to avoid the Allied air offense, made even more arduous and tiring due to the lack of means of transport and the prohibitive weather conditions, with heavy snowfalls that delayed the arrival on the line. However, there were many divisions in the Division that remained in the Parma area, from military hospitals to divisional warehouses, from the garrisons intended for the control of the route S.S. 62 of the Cisa to those intended for the protection of the Parma - Pontremoli railway line. Only towards the end of January began the exchange of deliveries between the Commands.

Gunners of the 2nd Regiment in the rear of Gothic line, note the *MG-42* and the huge supply of ammunition carried by the two soldiers (*Viziano*).

Bersaglieri of the 2nd Regiment on the *Gothic Line* (*Viziano*).

On the Garfagnana's front, the units of *"Italia"* replaced the *"Monterosa"*, *"San Marco"* and *148. German Infanterie-Division* units. The sector of the Apuan Alps and the Serchio Valley thus became the responsibility of the *"Italia"*, to which the *"Intra"* Battalion and the *"Bergamo"* Artillery Group of the *"Monterosa"* remained, with the task of helping the insertion of the Bersaglieri in line, very tried and discouraged joints at the front.

Bersaglieri of Division "*Italia*" with 81mm mortar, intent on stripping the grenades (*Viziano*).

Machine-gun nest of the 3rd Battalion / 1st Regiment of '*Italia*' in Le Tese on the Garfagnana front (*Viziano*).

Between the 24th and 26th of January, the Division was visited by the Duce, who wanted to see for himself the state of the Bersaglieri and try to lift the morale of the soldiers. In addition to the Ozzano Division Headquarters, Mussolini also visited some principals, inspected the units of the Collecchio area, in Pontremoli and near Aulla, and then returned to Gargnano. From 4th to 11th February the Americans launched Operation "*Fourth Term*", with a diversionary attack in the Serchio Valley and the main attack in the coastal sector of Versilia, with the aim of overcoming the coastal resistance line and reaching Massa, thus disrupting the Massa Rigel which prevented it from reaching the La Spezia stronghold. This was the first real test of fire for the Bersaglieri of the "*Italia*", even if only one sector was of their competence, as the line was still defended by Alpini and Marò joined the new arrivals to gain experience. At the end of the American offensive the positions remained practically unchanged, but this thanks to the veterans of the "*Monterosa*" and the "*San Marco*" who contributed, with the German and Italian reserve units, to restore the leaks that were opened due to the collapse of some departments of the 2nd Battalion of the 1st Regiment,

collapse caused by the inexperience of war of the Bersaglieri and the poor quality of some officers. Having passed this test and completed the replacement with the previous on-line units, the Bersaglieri of "*Italia*" provided good evidence, demonstrating their quality and recovering confidence in their means during the subsequent stay at the front.

Intense close-up of a young Bersagliere of the 2nd Regiment. On the helmet bears the new insignia, representing a republican eagle, which was to be adopted on all military helmets of the Republican National Army, replacing the royal specialty insignia (*Viziano*).

Communication between the positions of "*Italia*" Division, often distant from each other, on the *'Gothic'* front was vital. Line guard is repairing a telephone cable (*Viziano*).

Bersaglieri of "*Italia*" Division transport ammunition to the front line, wearing makeshift camouflage garments (*Viziano*).

The Divisional Command was deployed to Camporgiano, formerly the headquarters of the previous "*Monterosa*" Command, while, starting from 21st February, General Carloni summarized the Division Command. When the Allied final offensive began in April 1945, the Division remained firmly established on its positions despite having its sides uncovered, due to the retreat of the German Divisions which were forced to yield to the pressure of the Allied troops. From April 10th, a series of interventions were arranged between General Carloni and General Fretter-Pico, commander of the *148. Infanterie-Division*, whose goal was the withdrawal of the units towards the bank of the Po through the Passo del Cerreto, to Reggio Emilia, and through the Passo della Cisa to Parma, also collecting the units coming from La Spezia.

Bersaglieri patrol of "*Italia*" Division, on patrol on the front of the "*Gothic*" Line. The soldier in the foreground wears an Italian curtain, facing the inside, to make himself less visible in the snow.

A German *IG18 75/10* howitzer is placed in position by *Bersaglieri* on the "*Gothic*" Line (*Viziano*).

To safely carry out this folding, a series of defensive strongholds were set up with the task of stopping the Allied avant-garde advancing along the coast and towards the hinterland behind the Serchio Valley. Two Combat Groups were therefore established, called "*Gruppo Ferrario*" and "*Gruppo Zelli-Jacobuzzi*" from the name of the respective Commanders, who had the task of acting as rearguard, to delay as much as possible the advance of the Allies. The fall back towards the Po Valley was heavily opposed by continuous bombardments, which caused heavy losses in men, vehicles, quadrupeds and wagons, and in some areas the partisans made their appearance by sniping. But the action of the Fighting Groups was particularly harsh, as they opposed the Allied attacks as long as they had strength. The fights sustained on the Colle Musatello and on the quotas of Viano are remarkable, where on the 22nd the 1st Company of the "*Mameli*" Battalion, of the "*Ferrario* Group", and of San Terenzo and Ceserano from the "*Zelli-Jacobuzzi Group*" were decimated. The wards were concentrated at Fornovo Taro, the last fight took place on the 28th, with the "*Ferrario Group*" that tried to overcome the Taro to break through the Allied lines and continue the retreat, an attempt rejected by the preponderant opposing forces. On April 29th, 1945, the "*Italia*" Division surrendered to the Brazilians of the F.E.B. receiving the Honours of war.

Divisional Structure

Commander: General Giardina, then Colonel i.g.s. Mario Carloni, then Colonel

Bersagliere of "*Italia*" Division assigned to a German *IG18* howitzer 75/10 (Viziano).

Two Bersaglieri of "*Italia*" Division on the Garfagnana front (*Viziano*).

i.g.s. Guido Manardi (Brigadier General since 19th August 1944), and finally Brigade General (Division General since 22 February 1945) Mario Carloni.

1st Bersaglieri Regiment
Regimental Command Company
Light Column
I Battalion
II Battalion
III Battalion
107th Tank Hunters Company

2nd Bersaglieri Regiment
Regimental Command Company
Light Column
I Battalion
II Battalion
II Battalion
108th Tank Hunters Company

4th Artillery Regiment
Regimental Command Battery
Light Column
I 75/13 Howitzers Group (on Group Command Battery e 3 Batteries)
II 75/27 Guns Group (on Group Command Battery e 2 Batteries)
III 149/19 Howitzers Heavy Group (on Group Command Battery e 3 Batteries)
IV Group (o Group Command Battery e 2 Batteries)

IV Exploring Group
Command Unit
1st Light Squadron
2nd Light Squadron
3rd Heavy Squadron

Divisional Units
IV Pioneers Battalion
IV Battalion Connections
IV Transport Battalion (5 transport columns and 1 warehouse)
CIV Complements Battalion (kept in a square position)
4th Divisional Anti-tank Company
Health Department on:
104th Healthcare Company
4th Healthcare Company
IV Surgical Core

Bersaglieri of "*Italia*" supply division supervise the ammunition boxes (*Viziano*).

In January 1945, the Duce visited the units of "*Italia*" Division deployed along the Gothic Line.

IV Ambulances Platoon
Administration Unit on:
Administration Company
Bakers Company
Butchers Company
Veterinary Company
Workshop Company
Subsistence Company
4th e 7th G.N.R.'s Sections
Military Tribunal
Divisional Deposit

Division Staff

In June 1944 a document reported a total of 14,183 soldiers, of which 3,720 former military prisoners, 9,902 flowed from Italy and 561 already in the area. At the 1st of September 1944 the new armament tables included: 461 officers, 1,864 non-commissioned officers and 9,047 troops, for a total of 11,367 military personnel, while the real situation presented a Division force of 11,960 men, with a surplus of officers and NCOs. The organic situation on February 28th, 1945 shows a table with a total of 10,962 Italians and 1,237 Germans including officers, non-commissioned officers, troops, interpreters and civil personnel, and a staff of 8,831 Italians and 1,188 Germans.

Weapons

The individual and divisional armament was a mixture of German and Italian material, there were Mauser 98k and model 91, *Breda* 30 light machine guns, *MG-42* and *Breda* 37 heavy machine guns, the guns were Italian and German. The mortars were 81 mm Italian and 80 mm German. The situation with regard to the supply of cannons and howitzers was very difficult. The Artillery Groups were equipped with 75/27 guns, 75/13 Italian howitzers and 149/19; at the arrival in Italy the 75/27 guns were replaced with 75/18 howitzers. In the weapons tables there were also 10 guns 7.5 IG18, 4 guns 15 SIG35 and 17 guns 7.5 Pak 40. In reality, on January 25th, 1945, the Division Commander complained of the presence of a single piece of 15, the lack of light infantry guns, replaced by 3 cannons of 65/17 without means of pointing, therefore useless, leftovers of 1st World War, while it did not mention the presence of the anti-tanks. It should be noted that the 149/19 howitzers of the III Group, were withdrawn a few days before reaching the line, when they were tried it was noticed that they were without liquid in the hydraulic recoil brakes, they had to spend many days before being able to make the pieces working. *Panzerfaust* were also included.

Vehicles

The "*Italia*" Division was the one that suffered the most from vehicle shortages, only the II Battalion / 1st Regiment was motorized, even the quadrupeds were largely insufficient.

The situation on January 25th, 1945 was as follows:

Vehicles: in organic 676, actually present 123 (deficiency 553)
Quadrupeds: foreseen 4,104, actually present 1,281 (deficiency 2,720)
Carts: foreseen 603, actually present 142 (deficiency 461)

On February 28th, the situation of quadrupeds was as follows: foreseen 4,684, actually present 1,823 (deficiency 2,861)

For the quadrupeds the situation was serious not only for the shortage that varied between 60 and 70%, but also for the characteristics of the animals, both the horses and the mules were of small size and unsuitable for towing of heavy loads. This fact also stemmed from the decision of the Germans who, before the division returned from Germany, recovered 416 draft horses to be assigned to their units in formation, trusting in the reintegration of the staff once they arrived in Italy. Particularly serious was the situation of the tractors for howitzers of the III Group of Artillery, instead of the Breda they had been assigned to the old Pavesi P4, absolutely unsuitable for their scarce reach and for little efficiency. The shortage of trucks was very serious, out of 225 in the workforce there were 31, of which half inefficient. The considerable number of vehicles out of use was motivated by the total lack of workshops, none of the 12 planned was present.

Losses

They have been identified 481 deads, of which 19 are unknown, and 21 were shot for desertion or theft, among these 3 are unknown. These are Fallen on the front of the Garfagnana and in other areas where the Division's units have operated or stopped.

Bibliography
Paolo Crippa – Carlo Cucut, "*Bersaglieri's Units Of Italian Social Republic*", Soldiershop Publishing

A Prussian General in the Waffen-SS
A Biographical Chronology of *Generaloberst der Waffen-SS* Paul Hausser

by Michael D. Miller
with Translation Assistance from Gary Costello

SS-Gruppenführer und Generalleutnant der Waffen-SS Paul Hausser in the late Summer of 1941.

A postwar-autographed portrait of Paul Hausser (*Roger Bender Collection*).

Karl Georg *Paul* ("Papa") Hausser
ᛋᛋ-Oberst-Gruppenführer und Generaloberst der Waffen- ᛋᛋ

Born: 07.10.1880 in Brandenburg an der Havel/Regierungsbezirk Potsdam/Provinz Mark Brandenburg.

Died: 21.12.1972 in Ludwigsburg / Württemberg. His funeral ceremony, held in Ludwigsburg on 28.12.1972, was attended by over 2,000 people, with the eulogy delivered by former *SS-Brigadeführer und Generalmajor der Waffen*-SS Otto Kumm (final commander of *1. SS-Pz.Div. "Leibstandarte SS Adolf Hitler"*).

NSDAP-Nr.: 4.138.779 (Joined 01.05.1937)
SS-Nr.: 239.795 (Joined 15.11.1934)

Promotions

20.03.1899: *Leutnant (mit Patent vom 20.03.1899)*
19.08.1909: *Oberleutnant (mit Patent vom 19.08.1909)*
01.10.1913: *Hauptmann i. G. (mit Patent vom 01.10.1913)*
22.03.1918: *Major (mit Patent vom 22.03.1918; 01.02.1922:* Granted *RDA vom 22. 03.1918)*
01.04.1923: *Oberstleutnant (mit RDA vom 15.11.1922)*
01.11.1927: *Oberst (mit RDA vom 01.07.1927)*
01.02.1931: *Generalmajor (mit RDA vom 01.02.1934)*
31.10.1932: *Charakter als Generalleutnant*
01.11.1933: *Landesführer der SA-Reserve I*
01.03.1934: *SA-Standartenführer*
15.11.1934: *SS-Standartenführer (mit Patent vom 01.11.1934)*
01.07.1935: *SS-Oberführer*
22.05.1936: *SS-Brigadeführer*
01.06.1938: *SS-Gruppenführer*
19.11.1940: *Generalleutnant der Waffen-SS*
01.10.1941: *SS-Obergruppenführer und General der Waffen-SS*
01.08.1944: *SS-Oberst-Gruppenführer und Generaloberst der Waffen-SS*

Career

ca. 1887-00.00.1890: Attended *Volksschule* and *Gymnasium* in Brandenburg an der Havel.

00.00.1890-00.00.1892: Attended *Realgymnasium* in Stettin (due to the posting of his father to that city).

00.00.1892-00.00.1896: Attended the *Kadettenvoranstalt Köslin* (Pommern).

00.00.1896-00.03.1899: Attended the *Haupt-Kadettenanstalt Berlin-Lichterfelde* (graduated *Oberprima*).

20.03.1899-01.10.1903: Commissioned and assigned to *Infanterie-Regiment Nr. 155* (Garrison: Ostrowo/Provinz Posen; redesignated *7. Westpreußische Infanterie-Regiment Nr. 155*, 27.01.1902). *Ranglisten* for the regiment indicate the following specific assignments (dates given are those of *Rangliste* publication; he held these posts as of those dates):

Zugführer in *6. Kompanie*: [02.05.1899]
Zugführer in *7. Kompanie*: [07.05.1900]
Zugführer in *1. Kompanie*: [01.06.1901]
Zugführer in *6. Kompanie*: [06.05.1903]

01.10.1903-00.00.1906: *Bataillonsadjutant* of *II. Bataillon/7. Westpreußische Infanterie-Regiment Nr. 155*.

00.00.1906-01.10.1908: *Regimentsadjutant* of *7. Westpreußische Infanterie-Regiment Nr. 155*. Detached for training during this period to the *Militär-Turnanstalt*, Berlin and *Gewehrfabrik* (artillery factory) Spandau.

00.00.1907-00.00.1908: Preparation for the *Militärakademie*.

Autumn 1908: Passed entrance examination in Posen for the *Kriegsakademie*, Berlin.

01.10.1908-21.07.1911: Attended the *Kriegsakademie* in Berlin for training as a *Generalstabsoffizier* (general staff officer).

Autumn 1909: *Feldartillerie* training in Stettin.

Autumn 1910: Training with *Ulanen-Regiment Ulm*.

22.08.1911-15.09.1911: Detached to the *Kaiserlichen Marine* (Imperial Navy) in Kiel, participating in the Autumn fleet exercises in the western Baltic and the Kattegat aboard the battleship *S.M.S. "Schlesien"*.

00.10.1911-31.03.1912: Returned to service with *7.Westpreußische Infanterie-Regiment Nr. 155*.

22.03.1912-22.03.1914: Attached to the *Topographische Abteilung* (topographical department) in the *Großen Generalstabes* (with effect from 01.04.1912).

Summer 1912: Participated in a large-scale technical surveying exercise in the area of Ortelsburg-Gerdauen.

00.00.1912-00.00.1912: Assigned as *Leiter* of an *Eisenbahn-Abteilung* (railway detachment) for mobilization duties.

09.11.1912-00.00.191_: Underwent training as *Flugzeug-Beobachter* (aerial observer) with *Fliegerbataillon Döberitz*.

22.03.1914-01.08.1914 (?): Officially assigned to the *Topographische Abteilung* in the *Großen Generalstab*.

01.08.1914-27.01.1915: Assigned to the *Generalstab* of *6. Armee* (commanded by *Kronprinz*

Rupprecht von Bayern), employed as *Flugzeug-Beobachter* over the Western Front. During the opening months of the war, he participated in the following engagements:

08.-19.08.1914	Border defense combat in Lothringen (Lorraine)
20.-22.08.1914	Battle of Lothringen
22.08.-14.09.1914	Batty of Nancy-Epinal
26.-27.08.1914	Taking of Fort Manonviller
23.09.-06.10.1914	Battle of the Somme
02.-12.10.1914	Battle of Arras
07.-10.10.1914	Static combat west of St. Quentin
13.10.1914-23.01.1915	Static combat in Flanders and Artois
15.-28.10.1914	Battle of Lille
30.10.-24.11.1914	Battle of Ypres
14.-24.12.1914	December battle in French Flanders

27.01.1915-00.10.1915: Assigned as *2. Generalstabsoffizier (Ib)* to *Generalstab* of *VI. Armee-Korps* (Western Front). Temporarily posted during this period as a *Kompanieführer* in *Infanterie-Regiment "von Goeben" (2. Rheinisches) Nr. 28*.

Hauptmann i. G. **Hausser stands third from right in this 1915 group photo (***Max Williams***).**

00.10.1915-00.01.1918: Assigned to the *Generalstab* of *109. Infanterie-Division* on the Eastern Front, then as *1. Generalstabsoffizier (Ia)* in the *Marine-Dienststelle Libau* (Latvia).

16.02.1918-01.04.1918: Assigned as *Ia* to *Generalstab* of *I. Reserve-Korps*. Succeeded Major Jarosch. Succeeded by Major Hemmerich.

01.04.1918(?)-00.00.1918: Assigned as *Ia* to *Generalstab* of *Generalkommando z.b.V. 59*.

00.00.1918-00.00.1918: Assigned as *Ia* to the General Staff of the *Rumänischen Korps Focşani* (under General Alexandru Avarescu).

A formal portrait of *Oberstleutnant* Hausser, ca. 1927.

Generalmajor Hausser, ca. 1931.

00.01.1919-00.05.1919: Assigned to *Generalstab* of *V. Armee-Korps* as *Verbindungsoffizier* of *Generalkommando* (*V. Armee-Korps* HQ) attached to *Grenzschutz Ost* (Glogau/Schlesien).

00.05.1919-30.09.1919: Assigned as *Ia* to *Generalstab* of *Reichswehr-Brigade 5*.

01.10.1919-30.09.1920: Assigned as *Ia* to *Generalstab* of *Wehrkreiskommando II* (Stettin).

01.10.1920-00.00.1922: Assigned as *Ia* to the staff of *2. Division* (Stettin).

00.00.1922-31.03.1923: *Kompanieführer* in *Infanterie-Regiment 5* (Stettin).

01.04.1923-01.03.1925: *Kommandeur* of *III. Bataillon/4. (Preußisches) Infanterie-Regiment* (Deutsch-Krone).

01.03.1925-31.10.1927: *Chef des Stabes* of *Wehrkreiskommando II* and *2. Division* (Stettin).

01.11.1927-31.10.1928: Assigned as *Oberst beim Stab* to *10.(Sächsisches) Infanterie-Regiment* (Dresden).

01.11.1928-31.10.1930: *Kommandeur* of *10. (Sächsisches) Infanterie-Regiment*.

01.11.1930-31.01.1932: *Infanterieführer IV* (Magdeburg). Succeeded *Oberst* Adalbert von Taysen. Succeeded by *Oberst* Hans-Georg von Jagow.

31.01.1932: Retired from the *Reichswehr* as *Char. Generalleutnant*, possibly for political differences with other officers. Resided in Kleinmachow bei Berlin and appeared as a guest lecturer at *Friedrich-Wilhelms-Universität*, Berlin.

05.02.1933-31.10.1933: Joined the *"Stahlhelm" Bund*, assigned as *Landesführer* in Berlin-Brandenburg.

05.02.1933-00.04.1934: *Landesführer* of the *Reichskriegerbund* in Berlin-Brandenburg. Succeeded Franz von Stephani. Succeeded by Hermann Müller.

Generalmajor **Hausser, ca. 1931.**

01.11.1933-28.02.1934: Transferred to the *SA-Reserve I (SAR-I)* when the *"Stahlhelm"-Bund* was absorbed by that organization, assigned as *Führer (m.d.F.b.)* of *Oberlandesverband III* and the *Landesverband Berlin-Brandenburg* of *SA-Reserve I*.

01.03.1934-29.10.1934: *Führer* of *SAR-I-Brigade R 25 "Berlin-Brandenburg"*.

Summer 1934: During *SA* maneuvers in Friedrichsroda, Hausser met with an old regimental comrade, *SS-Brigadeführer* Paul Scharfe, who subsequently introduced him to *Reichsführer-SS* Heinrich Himmler.

01.11.1934: Discharged from the *SA*.

15.11.1934-01.07.1935: Joined the *SS-Verfügungstruppe, "mit den Vorarbeiten für die SS-Führerschule Braunschweig beauftragt"* (charged with preliminary work toward the establishment of the SS officer training school in Braunschweig, with effect from 01.11.1934). Himmler invited Hausser into the *SS* in order to examine the issue of training the militarized *SS* units, or *SS-Verfügungstruppe*.

01.07.1935-22.05.1936: *Kommandeur* of the *SS-Junkerschule Braunschweig* (with effect from 01.11.1934). First holder of this post. Succeeded by Friedemann Götze.

Hausser and two of his officers at *SS-Führerschule Braunschweig*, **1935. At right is Hausser's adjutant,** *SS-Sturmbannführer* **Walter Neumann.**

01.08.1935-05.05.1937: *Inspekteur der SS-Junkerschulen Braunschweig & Bad Tölz*. First holder of this post. Succeeded by Walter Schmitt.

22.05.1936-30.09.1936: *Chef* of *Amt I* (*Führungsamt*) in the *SS-Hauptamt*. Succeeded August Heißmeyer. Succeeded by Hermann Cummerow.

SS-Oberführer Hausser and his then-Chief of Staff, *SS-Sturmbannführer* Matthias Kleinheisterkamp (left) during training exercises at *SS-Führerschule* Braunschweig, 1935.

Hausser and Kleinheisterkamp, 1935.

01.10.1936-10.08.1939: *Inspekteur der SS-Verfügungstruppe*. First holder of this post. Tension eventually grew between Hausser and Josef ("Sepp") Dietrich over who was to control the militarized *SS*. Dietrich refused to acknowledge that Hausser as Inspector of the *SS-VT* had any say in the affairs of the *Leibstandarte-SS*. This tension culminated in May 1938 with Hausser's threat to resign. The cause of this state of affairs was Dietrich's refusal to provide officers and men of the *Leibstandarte* for the newly formed *"Der Führer" Regiment* of the *SS-VT*. Nothing changed, however Dietrich essentially agreed to disagree with Hausser and tension between the two eased in Summer 1938.

01.05.1937: Joined the *NSDAP*.

25.07.1939 - 09.10.1939: *Verbindungsoffizier*

(liaison officer) of the *SS-VT* attached to the divisional staff of *Panzerverband Ostpreussen* (redesignated *Panzer-Division "Kempf"*, 10.08.1939). This unit was created 25.07.1939 and commanded by the former commander of *4. Panzer-Brigade*, *Generalmajor* Werner Kempf.

SS-Oberführer **Hausser** **observes training exercises from horseback, ca. 1936.**

It consisted of an Army *Panzer-Regiment*, *SS-Standarte "Deutschland"*, the *SS-Artillerie-Regiment*, and various other Army and *SS-VT* units. It served under *I.* and *III. Armee-Korps* during the Polish Campaign, returned to Berlin 03.10.1939, and was disbanded 09.10.1939.

25.09.1939: Participated in the state funeral for *Generaloberst* Werner Freiherr von Fritsch (killed in action in Poland, 22.09.1939), Berlin.

10.10.1939-01.04.1940:
Aufstellungskommandeur der SS-V-Division (formation commander of the *SS-Division Verfügungstruppe*) at the *Truppenübungsplatz Brdy-Wald* bei Pilsen (in the area of Würzburg as of 30.11.1939 and in the area of Münster as of 24.01.1940). This was the formation staff used in the creation of the *SS-V- Division*, consisting of *SS-Standarten "Germania"*, *"Deutschland"*, and *"Der Führer"*.

01.04.1940-14.10.1941:
Kommandeur of the *SS-V-Division* (redesignated *SS-Division "Deutschland"*, 01.12.1940 and

SS-Brigadeführer **Hausser** **(right) speaks to** *SS-Gruppenführer* **Ernst-Heinrich Schmauser, ca. 1937.**

SS-Division (mot.) "Reich" on 21.12.1940) in the Western Campaign, in the occupation of the Netherlands, and in the invasions of Yugoslavia and Russia. Relinquished command to his senior regimental commander, Willi Bittrich, due to severe wounds sustained on 14.10.1941 (see entry for that date, below). In a performance evaluation dated 11.01.1942, *General der Panzertruppe* Heinrich von Vietinghoff-Scheel (*Kommandierender General, XXXXVI. Panzer-Korps*) assessed him as follows:

SS-Gruppenführer **Hausser during the early stages of the Western Campaign, May 1940.**

The divisional commander takes notes during a pause in the advance, May 1940. Note the British prisoner in the background.

Brief assessment (personality value, conduct before the enemy, official performance): Strong, hard person; as a senior Chef, thoroughly well trained in tactics; despite his age physically extremely efficient [and] prepared to utilize himself to the utmost. The high quality of his Division was made possible through his confident and purposeful leadership. In attack as in defense equally good performance; the most difficult situations, as they often turned out, were mastered with superior strength. Very caring and comradely. How does he fulfill his present position? Very well. Next possible utilization: Perfectly suitable as the Commanding General of a Panzerkorps. (SS-Personalakte Hausser)

In October 1941, two senior Panzer formation leaders had also recommended Hausser for command of a Panzer-Korps, as follows:

03.10.1941:
Gen. Kdo. XXIV Panzerkorps
The Kommandierender General
Regarding Gruppenführer Hausser
to <u>Panzergruppe 2.</u>
During the assignment of the SS-Division "Reich" to the XXIV A.K., even in difficult situations Gruppenführer Hausser led in a particularly brave, deliberate, with complete confident and personally. The fighting quality of the Division, as led by him, was exceptionally good. He supported the Korps leadership through suitable proposals. In my opinion, he is more than capable and suitable to take on the leadership role of a Panzer Generalkommando [Corps HQ]. [Signed] Frhr. von G e y r.

07.10.1941:
Oberkommando der 2. Panzerarmee
Oberbefehlshaber to <u>Heeresgruppe Mitte.</u>
SS-Gruppenführer, Generalleutnant H a u s s e r *led his Division in an especially brave and confident manner. The military attitude of the troops and their combat performance also stood out favorably due to the influence of the divisional commander. Suitable to be the Kommandierenden General of a Panzerkorps.*
[Signed] G u d e r i a n.
[Acknowledged by *Generalfeldmarschall* Fedor von Bock, *Oberbefehlshaber* of *Heeresgruppe Mitte*]
(SS-Personalakte Hausser)

SS-Gruppenführer Hausser (wearing the 1939 clasp to the 1914 Iron Cross First Class that he received on 17 May 1940) with an unidentified *SS-Oberführer* (*Photo by SS-Kriegsberichter Paul Augustin*).

The *Ritterkreuz* award ceremony for *SS-Untersturmführer* Ludwig Kepplinger (*SS-KB Augustin*).

00.06.1940-15.08.1940: *Chef* of the *Kommandoamt der SS* in the *SS-Hauptamt*. This became *Amt I* of the newly formed *SS-Führungshauptamt*, headed by Hans Jüttner, on 15.08.1940.

14.10.1941: Severely wounded by shrapnel on the *Rollbahn* before Istra near Gjatsch on the Borodino, losing part of his right upper jaw and being blinded in the right eye.

14.10.1941 - 28.05.1942: Hospitalization and convalescence. On 05.05.1942, he reported to the *Reichsführer-SS* that his health was improving.

28.05.1942 - 01.06.1942: *Aufstellungskommandeur* (formation commander) of the *SS-Generalkommando* (Corps HQ) at *Truppenübungsplatz Bergen*.

01.06.1942 - 28.06.1944: *Kommandierender General* of *SS-Generalkommando (Panzer)*. Redesignated *I. SS-Panzer-Korps*, 28.04.1943, then to *II. SS-Panzer-Korps* on 01.06.1943 (renumbered to allow for the raising of the *Leibstandarte SS* to corps status). This corps was briefly upgraded to *1. SS-Pz.Armee* in the Autumn of 1943. First holder of this post. Succeeded by Willi Bittrich. At Kharkov, he directly disobeyed Hitler's orders and withdrew his troops from the city to save lives; though he later recaptured the city in March 1943, he received no official recognition for the effort.

After Operation *"Zitadelle"* at Kursk, the *II. SS-Pz.Korps* was transferred to northern Italy under Rommel's *Heeresgruppe B*. While there, in connection with *"Fall Achse"*, Hausser's formation was tasked with disarming members of the Italian armed forces (who were deported to the Reich for forced labor). The formation also participated in a major anti-partisan operation in Slovenia (20.09.1943-20.11.1943). It was then transferred, in December, to France. From March to mid-June 1944, it was engaged on the Eastern Front, then transferred back to France to resist the Allied advance through Normandy.

Culenborg in The Netherlands, 04.09.1940: Hausser salutes during a parade in honor of *SS-Obersturmführer* Fritz Vogt (standing before him) who had just received the *Ritterkreuz* (as *Kompanieführer of 2. Kompanie/SS-V Aufklärungs-Abteilung*).

28.06.1944-01.09.1944: *Oberbefehlshaber* of *7. Armee* (*m.d.F.b.* until 01.08.1944, then appointed to permanent command). Succeeded *Generaloberst* Friedrich Dollmann who committed suicide on 28.06.1944. Succeeded, due to wounds sustained 20.08.1944 (see below), by *General der Panzertruppe* Erich Brandenburger. Of his appointment, *Generalleutnant a. D.* Hans Speidel wrote:

Without further consultation with Rommel, SS-Obergruppenführer Hausser, commander of the II SS Panzer Corps, was appointed to succeed Dollmann. Hausser had to leave his corps at the very moment when it was to lead the attack against the enemy front at Caen. Hausser had served in the Army and the General Staff, but he had gone into the SS at an early date. He was soldierly, had driven and marked courage, but was difficult to fathom in political matters, a veritable Janus. His appointment was received with mixed feelings; he was younger in service than many commanding generals... (Speidel, *Invasion 1944*, pp. 102-103).

The *Reichsführer-SS* during a visit to Hausser's Division, June 1940. Left to right: Werner Ostendorff, Heinrich Himmler, Paul Hausser, and Karl Wolff (*Roger Bender*).

10.07.1944: Appointed to head the *Kommandoamt der Waffen-SS* in the *SS-Führungshauptamt* (posting cancelled due to the military situation in Normandy).

16.08.1944-17.08.1944: *Führer* (*m.d.F.b.*) of *Heeresgruppe B*. Temporarily assigned due to the suicide of *Generalfeldmarschall* Günther von Kluge. Succeeded by *Generalfeldmarschall* Walter Model.

21.08.1944: Severely wounded in the right side of the skull by shrapnel during the breakout from the Argentan-Falaise pocket and evacuated aboard an armored personnel carrier.

00.08.1944-21.01.1945 (?): Hospitalization and convalescence in various medical facilities, including the *Lazarett* in Greifswald, due to wounds sustained 20.08.1944.

23.01.1945-29.01.1945: *"beauftragt mit der stellvertretenden Führung"* (charged with acting leadership) of *Heeresgruppe Oberrhein*. Succeeded Heinrich Himmler.

Paul Hausser speaks to his officers and men during training operations, Spring 1941 (*Photos by SS-Kriegsberichter Paul Augustin*).

08.08.1941: Hausser is decorated with the *Ritterkreuz* by *General der Panzertruppe* Heinrich von Vietinghoff-Scheel (far right).

Paul Hausser in his command post, 1941.

28.01.1945-03.04.1945: *Befehlshaber* of *Heeresgruppe G* (consisting of *1.* and *19. Armee*). Succeeded *Generaloberst* Johannes Blaskowitz. He was dismissed from command due to a disagreement with Hitler. On 10.02.1945, he issued the following order: *The combination of depleted units, and the deployment of youthful and inadequate reinforcements, have had an untoward effect on morale. Moreover, the front is so wide that the influence of officers and Party officials is no longer as effective as it might be. Hence the danger of desertion has increased, and preventive measures are* *urgently needed. One of our Armies has accordingly asked that the measures regarding the arrest of family-hostages be made known to the troops. It should, however, be remembered that the threat of arresting dependents has lost much of its force, particularly when the families concerned are in enemy-occupied territory.*

[signed] *HAUSSER* - Oberbefehlshaber Heeresgruppe G
(Hans Dollinger, *The Decline and Fall of Nazi Germany and Imperial Japan*, p. 63)

Informal portraits of Paul Hausser after receiving the *Ritterkreuz*.

Paul Hausser with *Ritterkreuz*.

On 20.03.1945, Hausser met with *Reichsminister* Albert Speer, with whom he reached an agreement that Hitler's *"Nero-Befehl"* (concerning a "scorched earth" policy in Germany) should not be implemented. Speer writes:

It took until midnight for us to reach the army headquarters, situated in a wine-growing village in the Palatinate. SS General Hausser was more sensible in the interpretation of insane orders than his Commander in Chief [Generalfeldmarschall Albert Kesselring]. Hausser thought that the ordered evacuation could not possibly be carried out and that blowing up the bridges would be irresponsible. (Speer, *Inside the Third Reich*, p. 559)

04.04.1945: Transferred to the *Führerreserve*.

00.04.1945-09.05.1945: Attached as *General z.b.V.* to the staff of *Oberbefehlshaber Südwest* (*Generalfeld.*Albert Kesselring).

in World War Two 1939-1945

Hausser, wearing a heavy, fur-lined coat, stands in the turret of an armored vehicle, not long before the 14.10.1941 injury that resulted in the loss of his right eye and part of his jaw.

06.05.1945 - 09.05.1945: *Sonderbeauftragter für Sicherheit und Ordnung beim Stab des Oberbefehlshabers Süd* (Special Representative for Security and Order attached to the Staff of Commander-in-Chief South).

Postwar Confinement & Activities

09.05.1945-00.01.1948: Surrendered to U.S. troops at Zell am See/Österreich, then held in U.S. captivity for two-and-a-half years. As of 24.05.1945, he was under interrogation at the U.S. 7th Army Interrogation Center in Augsburg, where, in a Final Interrogation Report dated 09.07.1945, the following comments were made by *Major* Paul Kubala, commander of the facility:

Source is a firm believer in Hitler's theories, and attempted to justify most of the Fuehrer's deeds, but he talked freely on military matters. Formerly a Prussian general in the Army, source stressed the fact that he was primarily a military leader and not a politician... (*Interrogation Records Prepared for War Crimes Proceedings at Nuernberg, 1945-1947/OCCPAC Interrogation Transcripts and Related Records: Hausser, Paul;* Publication Number M1270, Record Group RG238)

Interned in 20 different camps, including the "War Crimes" Camp in Dachau, the Oberursel internment camp near Frankfurt am Main (where he worked with the U.S. Army's Military Historical Division), a camp in Nürnberg (while he appeared as a defense witness regarding the *Waffen-SS* before the International Military Tribunal, 05.-06.08.1946), and finally at *Lager Neustadt-Allendorf* near Marburg until the start of 1948.

00.01.1948: Placed under automatic detention by German authorities at *Lager Neustadt-Allendorf.*

00.01.1948-Summer 1948: Tried by a de-Nazification court and sentenced to 2 years' labor camp. Sentence upheld by the *Zentralberufungskammer Nordwürttemberg,* 00.07.1949.

00.00.1951-21.12.1972: Cofounder (with Herbert Otto Gille and Otto Kumm) and *Erster Vorsitzender* (first chairman) of the *Hilfsgemeinschaft auf Gegenseitigkeit der Angehörigen der ehemaligen Waffen-SS* (*HIAG*, Mutual Aid Society for Members of the Former *Waffen-SS*), remaining in that post until his death (succeeded by Willi Bittrich). He was known, unofficially and affectionately, as *"Der Senior"* by the membership of *HIAG*.

Hausser listens to a report from *SS-Hauptsturmführer* Fritz Klingenberg, *Kommandeur* of the "Reich" Division's *Kradschützen-Bataillon*, ca. September 1941. Between them is the *1. Generalstabsoffizier (Ia)* of *"Reich"*, Werner Ostendorff.

Hausser with General von Vietinghoff-Scheel.

24.09.1951: Selected, along with Herbert Otto Gille, for the provisional presidency of the newly formed *Verband deutscher Soldaten* (Association of German Soldiers).

06.04.1962: Establishment, in Ettlingen (Baden), of the *Sozialwerk Paul Hausser e.V.* by former *SS-Brigadeführer* Karl Cerff.

07.10.1970: 90th birthday party, attended by numerous *Bundeswehr* officials and West German politicians, including *Generalleutnant* Albert Schnez (Inspector of the *Bundeswehr*), *Generalmajor* (*Luftwaffe*) Willi Wagenknecht, *Ministerpräsident* Hans Filbinger (a representative of the *CDU*). Several *Bundestag* delegates sent written birthday greetings. On the same date, *SS-Obergruppenführer und General der Waffen-SS a. D.* Wilhelm Bittrich appeared as the main speaker at a ceremony honoring Hausser in Ludwigsburg.

Paris, 21.06.1942: Hausser, recently recovered from his 14.10.1941 wounds, returns a salute (*Bundesarchiv*).

September 1942: Hausser and Ostendorff during the test drive of a *Schwimmwagen*. Driving the amphibious vehicle is *SS-Hauptsturmführer* Heinz Meiswinkel (TFK, *Technischer Führer für das Kraftfahrwesen*) of *Kradschützen-Bataillon 2*.

Kharkov, during Himmler's 26.-27.04.1943 inspection of Hausser's *SS-Panzer-Korps*. Left to right: Walter Krüger (Kdr., *SS-Panzer-Grenadier-Division "Das Reich"*), Reichsführer-SS Himmler and Paul Hausser.

16.10.1972: Last public appearance, attending a veterans' meeting of *2. SS-Panzer-Division "Das Reich"* in Bad Aibling.

28.12.1972: Funeral in Ludwigsburg. The memorial address was read by *SS-Brigadeführer und Generalmajor der Waffen-SS a. D.* Otto Kumm.

07.10.1980: Speech delivered in München to honor Hausser's 100th birthday by the honorary chairman of the *Verband deutscher Soldaten*, *Bundeswehr-Generalleutnant a. D.* Gerhard Matzky.

A postwar-autographed unposed photo of Paul Hausser as *SS-Obergruppenführer und General der Waffen-SS* (*Roger Bender Collection*).

A postwar-signed image of Paul Hausser.

Published Works

Waffen-SS im Einsatz (Waffen-SS in Action) (1949)

Aus der Geschichte der Waffen-SS (Sonderdruck der DSZ, 1952)

Soldaten wie andere auch. Der Weg der Waffen-SS (Soldiers Like Any Other-The Path of the Waffen-SS), Munin Verlag (1966)

Decorations & Awards

26.08.1944: *Schwertern zum Ritterkreuz des Eisernen Kreuzes* (90.) as *SS-Oberst-Gruppenführer und Generaloberst der Waffen-SS* and *Oberbefehlshaber* of *7. Armee/Oberbefehlshaber West*, Western Front. Personally presented by Hitler at *Führer HQ "Wolfsschanze"* (Rastenburg/Ostpreußen), 26.08.1944. Awarded on the basis of the following *Vorschlag* (proposal), dated 23.08.1944 and submitted via telegram:

I hereby request the presentation of the Swords to the Oakleaves of the Knight's Cross of the Iron Cross to SS-Oberst-Gruppenführer und Generaloberst Hausser. SS-Oberst-Gruppenführer und Generaloberst Hausser, Oberbefehlshaber of the 7th Armee, assumed command of the Army in the most difficult situation. He constantly led from the front and carried out daily visits to the troops under the heaviest of enemy action. A decisive decision to attack Avranches using the extracted Panzer units only failed due to superior enemy air support. Even though there was a risk of encirclement and despite the possibility of withdrawal, Generaloberst Hausser remained with his troops. In this manner, it was possible to influence the commanding generals until a breakout from the encirclement was carried out. Generaloberst Hausser took part in the breakthrough as part of the formation of II. Fallschirmjäger-Korps and broke out of the encirclement under heavy enemy artillery fire. He was severely wounded during the breakout. Generaloberst Hausser is especially worthy of the presentation of the Swords to the Oakleaves of the Knight's Cross, since in particular, during the breakout, he was a model example of bravery and determined leadership to all subordinated formations.

in World War Two 1939-1945

General Hausser in the commander's cupola of a Panzer III, 1943.

Paul Hausser Kdr of *II. SS-Panzer-Korps*.

Personnel records will be submitted subsequently [Signed] Model *Generalfeldmarschall und Oberbefehlshaber West.*

28.07.1943: *Eichenlaub zum Ritterkreuz des Eisernen Kreuzes* (261.) as *SS-Obergruppenführer und General der Waffen-SS* and *Kommandierender-General* of *II. SS-Panzer-Korps/4. Panzer-Armee,* Eastern Front. Personally presented by Hitler at *Führer HQ "Wolfsschanze"* (Rastenburg/Ostpreußen), 28.07.1943. Awarded on the basis of the following proposal signed by *Generaloberst* Hermann Hoth (*Oberbefehlshaber* of *4. Panzer-Armee*):

I hereby propose awarding Oakleaves to the Knight's Cross to the Commanding General of the II. SS-Panzerkorps, SS-Obergruppenführer und General der Waffen-SS Hausser, for multiple extraordinary achievements in the leadership of the troops during the attack operation north of Belgorod (Zitadelle). On the first day of the attack, 5 June, at noon the attack by the "Leibstandarte" faltered due to the overwhelming artillery fire from the heights at Shurawliny and south of Olchowka. The Commanding General at the front recognized the crisis and immediately issued extremely expedient orders. Almost all of the Corps' artillery was used to fight the enemy artillery and the entire VIII. Fliegerkorps was brought to bear onto the batteries. Realizing that now the attack of the Division Das Reich had to bring the necessary relief, he hurried further forward, ordered the Panzers of this Division to be deployed, and ordered the immediate attack of Division "Totenkopf", which, according to the original attack plan, was supposed to start later on the right rearward of Division "Das Reich". The success was resounding. The attack of the "Leibstandarte" through the deeply developed position regained momentum, the stronghold of Shurawliny was stormed from two sides, and in the evening the Corps stood in front of the second enemy position and began to clean up the enemy on the right flank of the Army. On the second day of attack, the II. SS-Panzerkorps had broken through the enemy's second position, when it was reported that a strong enemy tank force was approaching from Prochorowka. The Commanding General, who had hurried to the front, recognized the favorable situation. Although it was clear that the XXXXVIII. Panzer-Korps was still involved in a hard fight for the second position northeast of Olchowka and the action of the II. SS-Panzer-Korps was outflanked by this, the Commanding General decided to turn the mass of the Corps against Prochorowka in order to keep the enemy as far away from the battlefield as possible.

Hausser as Commanding General of the *SS-Panzer-Korps* **observing training exercises, 21.06.1943. Left to right:** *SS-Gruppenführer und Generalleutnant der Waffen-SS* **Walter Krüger** (*Kdr. SS-Panzer-Grenadier-Division "Das Reich"*), *SS-Obersturmbannführer* **Hans-Albin Freiherr von Reitzenstein** (*Kdr. SS-Panzer-Regiment 2*), **Hausser, and** *SS-Oberführer* **Werner Ostendorff** (*Chef des Generalstabes, Generalkommando SS-Panzer-Korps*) (*Photo by SS-Kriegsb.* **Willi Merz**).

Hausser Kdr of *II. SS-Pz.Korps.*

Leaving safeguards at Pokrowka, he himself led the Panzers of the "Das Reich" and "Leibstandarte" Divisions towards the road Lutschki - Prochorowka. In heavy tank battles it was possible to inflict heavy losses on the IInd Tank Corps and the Vth Guard Tank Corps, pushing them back the towards Prochorowka and therefore making it possible to conquer the high ground at Teterewino. On this day, 7 July, there were serious crises among the forces of the Division "Das Reich", left to cover the right flank near Teterewino, which was attacked from the East by the newly introduced VIth Tank Corps and the remains of the IInd Tank and Vth Guard Tank Corps. The enemy broke through the infantry of the Division "Das Reich" in several places in great depth with numerous tanks. The Commanding General, once again on the spot, maintained the tank advance to the west despite the threat of a breakthrough, and thanks to the tenacity of the SS-Panzergrenadiers spurred on by the presence of the Commanding General, it was possible *to finish the off the tanks which had penetrated in close combat and prevent the breakthrough. I hardly ever met Obergruppenführer Hausser at the advanced Corps command post during the 14-day operation, but always only at the front with the Divisions or returning from the troops. Despite his physical handicap due to previous severe injuries, he tirelessly led the troop from the front the whole day, providing the troops with drive and momentum even in difficult situations through his presence, courage and humor, whilst still keeping a firm grip on the Corps leadership.*

Rastenburg/Ostpreußen, 28.07.1943: *SS-Obergruppenführer und General der Waffen-SS* **Hausser receives the Oakleaves to the Knight's Cross from Adolf Hitler at** *Führer* **HQ "Wolfsschanze".**

Hausser at *Führer* HQ after receiving the Oakleaves.

As with the spring offensive on Charkow, Obergruppenführer Hausser has shown foresight in recognizing operational situations, integration into the overall situation and energy and bravery in the execution of combat operations and has once more distinguished himself as an unusually capable Commanding General. [Signed] Hoth *Generaloberst und Oberbefehlshaber* of 4. *Panzerarmee*

08.08.1941: *Ritterkreuz des Eisernen Kreuzes* as *SS-Gruppenführer und Generalleutnant der Waffen-SS* and *Kommandeur* of *SS-Division "Reich"/XXXXVI. Panzer-Korps/Panzergruppe 2/4. Panzer-Armee/Heeresgruppe Mitte,* Eastern Front. *"Vorschlagsliste Nr. 411 für die Verleihung des Ritterkreuzes des Eisernen Kreuzes"* dated 05.08.1941, which read: *Gruppenführer Hausser had already proven himself to be an excellent leader during the Western*

Campaign. Excellent tactical training, unreserved personal commitment, always intervening personally at the most dangerous locations, maximum confidence and calmness, and a tenacious will to master even the most difficult situations are what distinguish him. Decisive influence was gained by his leadership during the battles between Beresina and Dnieper. After crossing the Beresina, the SS-Div. 'Reich' received the order to attack on the left wing of the XXXXVI. Pz. Korps to relieve the 10. Pz. Div, which was under heavy pressure, and to advance with it rapidly via Belynichi on Shklov to the Djepr. In order to confront and destroy the enemy, who cleverly fought its way to the East, the Div. Kdr decided on the evening of 7.7.1941 to dispatch the reinforced Kradschtz. Btl. with the order to advance to Esmon, to confront the enemy at the Oslik sector and to close off the sector.

Two views of Hausser as *Oberbefehlshaber* of *7. Armee* with Erwin Rommel in Normandy, 1944.

Villebaudon, Normandy, on the afternoon of 14.07.1944. From left to right: Hausser, Rommel, and *General der Fallschirmtruppe* Eugen Meindl, *Kommandierender* General of II. Fallschirmjäger-Korps.

The mass of the Division was to attack the enemy frontally, hereby taking the northern flank. At Somry the enemy strongly resisted the reinforced SS-Rgt. "Der Führer". The Div. Kdr. Hastened to the front Btl. to gain a personal insight into the strength and structure of the enemy. When passing through the village, he was slightly injured by the shrapnel of a grenade which landed a few meters away from him, [yet] still he continued to lead the Division. By drawing on the mass of the available artillery, the Div. Kdr. succeeded in driving the attack forward in difficult forest terrain despite the stubborn resistance of the enemy. The opponent was the 100th Division (Moscow), one of the best Russian divisions. The skillful and energetic leadership of the Div. Kdr. succeeded in throwing back the enemy, which was attacking from all sides, and destroying most of them in what was extremely difficult terrain. The rapid advance from the Beresina to the Dnieper, while destroying the best Russian troops, created the precondition for the enemy being unable to organize the defense behind the Dnieper. This enabled the K [Panzergruppe Kleist] to cross the Dniepr quickly and the early deep follow-up of the 10. Pz. Div., which was of decisive importance for the overall operations. During the campaign in the West, the SS-Div. "Reich", under the leadership of Gruppenführer Hausser, took part in the following decisive actions:

16.07.1944, at Villebaudon in the area of St.-Lô, site of II. Fallschirmkorps headquarters. From left to right: *General der Fallschirmtruppe* Eugen Meindl (*Kommandierender General II. Fallschirmkorps*), Paul Hausser (*Oberbefehlshaber 7. Armee*), and *Generalleutnant Dipl.Ing.* Richard Schimpf (*Kommandeur 3. Fallchirmjäger-Division*). In the background, behind Schimpf, is *SS-Hauptsturmführer* Karl-Heinz Boska (Hausser's adjutant).

A very rare image of Paul Hausser with the rank of *SS-Oberst-Gruppenführer.*

a) In three days, the Division took the island of Walcheren alone in the battle against Dutch and French troops, and thus achieved the early surrender of the fortress of Antwerp, which was flanked by the capture of Vlissingen and became unusable as a port for the enemy.

b) In the Battle of Flanders, the Division fought as part of the Panzergruppe Kleist in the Nieppe forest against English troops who bravely defended it, taking the forest after 4 days of fighting, and thus played a decisive role in the encirclement of the English-French troops in Flanders.

c) During the advance of the Panzer troops to the plateau of Langres the Division had the task of securing the deep left flank of Gruppe Kleist. At the upper Seine it encountered the French troops returning from the Maginot Line to the southeast, attacked them in the area of Chatillon s. /Seine and destroyed them completely. In one day, 20,000 prisoners were taken by the division, 14 [artillery] batteries, and countless items of equipment were captured.

High-ranking German prisoners of war who were recruited to collaborate with the U.S. Army Military History unit. Left to right: *Generalmajor* Friedrich-Wilhelm von Mellenthin (*Chef des Generalstabes, 5. Panzer-Armee*), *General der Infanterie* Otto Hitzfeld (*Kommandierender General LXVII. Armee-Korps*), B. E. Croseclose (Historical Division U.S. Forces European Theater [USFET], Central Germany Sub-Section), *Generalleutnant* Fritz Bayerlein (*Führer LIII. Armee-Korps*), *General der Artillerie* Walther Lucht (*Kommandierender General XIII. Armee-Korps*), *Generalmajor* Rudolf-Christoph Freiherr von Gersdorff (*Chef des Generalstabes 7. Armee*), and *Lieutenant* J. F. Scoggin, Jr. (Chief, Central Germany Sub-Section, Historical Division USFET). Seated at left is Paul Hausser and beside him, *Generalmajor* Carl Wagener (*Chef des Generalstabes Heeresgruppe B*).

Paul Hausser and an unidentified fellow veteran, 1970.

Signed Vietinghoff
General der Panzertruppe and *Kommandierenden General* of *XXXXVI. Pz. Korps.*

The proposal was further endorsed by the *Oberbefehlshaber of Panzergruppe 2, Generaloberst* Heinz Guderian:

The Commander of Panzer Gruppe 2.
In the heavy battles between the Berisina and the Dnieper and then from the Dnieper to Jelnja, Guppenführer Hausser led his excellent troops with outstanding personal commitment, always remaining at the focal points of the battle, and without regard to the threat from the flanks and the rear, he led his excellent troops to decisive victories in difficult terrain and across several rivers.
The proposal is approved
[Signed] Guderian *Generaloberst.*

Subsequent endorsements were made by the *Panzer-Armee Oberbefehlshaber* (*Generalfeldmarschall* Günther von Kluge); the *Heeresgruppe Oberbefehlshaber* (*Generalfeldmarschall* Fedor von Bock); and the *Oberbefehlshaber des Heeres* (*Generalfeldmarschall* Walther von Brauchitsch).

27.01.1917: *Ritterkreuz des Kgl. Preußischen Hausordens von Hohenzollern mit Schwertern*
17.05.1940: *1939 Spange zum 1914 Eisernes Kreuz I. Klasse*
27.09.1939: *1939 Spange zum 1914 Eisernes Kreuz II. Klasse*
Winter 1915/16: *1914 Eisernes Kreuz I. Klasse*
07.09.1914: *1914 Eisernes Kreuz II. Klasse*

Paul Hausser and former *SS-Brigadeführer und Generalmajor der Waffen-SS* Kurt ("*Panzermeyer*") Meyer during a 2-day *Waffen-SS* reunion in Karlsberg, 27 July 1957.

SS-Oberst-Gruppenführer und Generaloberst der Waffen-SS a. D. Paul Hausser (1880 – 1972).

05.03.1915: *Ritterkreuz I. Klasse mit Schwertern des Kgl. Sächsischen Albrechts-Ordens I. Klasse*

28.07.1917: *Ritterkreuz des Militärischen Karl-Friedrich-Verdienstordens* (Baden)

07.09.1914: *Kgl. Bayerischer Militär-Verdienstorden IV. Klasse mit Schwertern und Krone*

26.02.1914: *Anhaltischer Friedrichkreuz*

11.07.1918: *k.u.k. Militär-Verdienstkreuz III. Klasse mit der Kriegsdekoration*

00.00.191_: *k.u.k. Orden der Eisernen Krone III. Klasse mit der Kriegsdekoration*

00.00.1912 (?): *Fliegerbeobachterabzeichen* (Preussen)

02.12.1914: *Ritterkreuz I. Klasse des Württembergischen Friedrichs-Ordens mit Schwertern*

09.05.1942: *Verwundetenabzeichen, 1939 in Silber*

ca. 1934: *Ehrenkreuz des Weltkrieges 1914-1918 mit Schwertern*

30.01.1943: *Goldenes Ehrenzeichen der NSDAP*

00.00.193_: *Ehrendolch der SS*

[01.12.1936]: *Ehrendegen des Reichsführers-SS*

[01.12.1936]: *Totenkopfring der SS*

00.00.193_: *SS-Zivilabzeichen* (Nr. 61.111)

16.12.1935: *Julleuchter der SS*

00.00.193_: *Ehrenwinkel für alte Kämpfer mit Stern*

Notes:

* Oldest son of *Premierlieutenant* Friedrich Wilhelm *Curt* Hausser (then assigned to *Füsilier-Regiment Nr. 35;* later rose to the rank of *Major*) and his wife Anna, née Otto.

* Religion: Lutheran until 00.00.1940, then left the church and declared himself *gottgläubig.*

* Married on 09.11.1912 to Elisabeth Gérard (born 18.07.1891 in Berlin, died 16.10.1978 in München). One daughter (Ingeborg Elisabeth, born 28.12.1913). Also buried in the Hausser family plot, his name appearing on the headstone with Paul and Elisabeth Hausser, is their son-in-law, Oberstleutnant a. D. Ernst Kurt *Hans-Joachim* Osterroht

(born 21.09.1909 in Frankfurt am Oder, died 00.00.1994). On 03.12.1943, *Major im Generalstab* Osterroht received the *Deutsches Kreuz in Gold* while assigned as *1. Generalstabsoffizier (Ia)* of *1. Flieger-Division.*

Sources

Bayerisches Hauptstaatsarchiv, München, Abteilung IV Kriegsarchiv: Excerpts from various *Kriegsranglisten* containing data on Paul Hausser's service with *6. Armee* in World War I.

Dollinger, Hans: *The Decline and Fall of Nazi Germany and Imperial Japan.* Bonanza, 1967.

Höhne, Heinz: *The Order of the Death's Head.* Martin Secker & Warburg, 1969.

National Archives and Records Administration, College Park, Maryland: *SS-Personalakte of Paul Hausser.* Microfilm document collection A3343SS.

- Interrogation Records Prepared for War Crimes Proceedings at Nuernberg, 1945-1947/OCCPAC Interrogation Transcripts and Related Records: Hausser, Paul; Publication Number M1270, Record Group RG238.

Nix, Philip: Biographical Notes from the archives of Mr. Nix, Birmingham, England.

Schulz, Andreas & Zinke, Dr. Dieter: *Die Generale der Waffen-SS und der Polizei 1933-1945, Band 2 (Hachtel-Kutschera).* Biblio-Verlag, 2005.

Speidel, Generalleutnant a. D. Hans: *Invasion 1944.* Henry Regnery Company, 1950.

SS-Personalkanzlei and SS-Personalhauptamt: *Dienstaltersliste der Schutzstaffel der NSDAP, Stand vom 1. Juli 1935.*

> *- Dienstaltersliste der Schutzstaffel der NSDAP, Stand vom 1. Dezember 1936.*
> *- Dienstaltersliste der Schutzstaffel der NSDAP, Stand vom 1. Dezember 1937.*
> *- Dienstaltersliste der Schutzstaffel der NSDAP, Stand vom 1. Dezember 1938.*
> *- Dienstaltersliste der Schutzstaffel der NSDAP, Stand vom 30. Januar 1942.*
> *- Dienstaltersliste der Schutzstaffel der NSDAP, Stand vom 20. April 1942.*
> *- Dienstaltersliste der Schutzstaffel der NSDAP, Stand vom 9. November 1944.*

Williams, Max: *The SS Leadership Corps, Volume I: A-E.* Ulric of England, 2004.

Yerger, Mark C.: *Waffen-SS Commanders-Augsberger to Kreutz.* Schiffer Military History, 1997.

Dedication

This article is dedicated to Roger James Bender (1940-2020), my publisher since 2001 and for over half a century one of the most tireless, talented, and creative forces in both the historical research and militaria collecting communities.

Hitler's Cossacks
by Sergio Volpe – Part 2

Helmuth von Pannwitz.

Cossack volunteer in German service.

Helmuth von Pannwitz

In the autumn of 1942, a cavalry officer of the 1st Army Corps, having already had experience with Cossack auxiliary units, suggested reorganizing all the Cossack units to use them in a more rational way. Son of a judge and old officer of the Hussars, Helmuth von Pannwitz, was born on October 14, 1898, in the family property of Botzanowitch in Upper Silesia, not far from the border with the Russian empire (Poland at that time was under Russian domination). He spent his childhood in this region, dividing his time between horseback riding and hunting. With his two brothers, he befriended the Cossacks who had settled on the other side of Lisswarthe, the river that marked the frontier with Tsarist Russia. This experience left a permanent mark on him. In 1914, at just fifteen, he entered the military school of Lichterfelde. When the war broke out, he was unable to reach the front because of his young age. However, in 1915, he managed to obtain the necessary authorization from his father to be part of a fighting unit. Flag bearer in a regiment of Uhlans, he served on the Russian front and in March 1915 he was promoted to Leutnant. In 1917, he was one of the first officers of his regiment to receive the Iron Cross First Class. Wounded during a fight in the Carpathians, he ended the war on General von Below's general staff, participating in the offensive on the Isonzo against the Italians. After the armistice, Pannwitz fought in a *Freikorp* in Silesia. In 1919, he was again wounded around Posen. Demobilized in March 1920, he spent a year in Hungary and then settled in Poland, as manager of a property of the Polish princess Radziwill.

Cossack volunteer in German service.

Cossack parade in Hitler's honor, 1942.

Returning to Germany in 1934, Pannwitz was reinstated in the army on January 1, 1935 and assigned to the 7th Cavalry Regiment stationed in Breslau in Silesia. Later, promoted to *Hauptmann*, he became squadron commander in the 2nd Cavalry Regiment of Augsburg, East Prussia. After the annexation of Austria, he was transferred to Vienna with the rank of major in the 11th Cavalry Regiment. In 1939, he took command of the reconnaissance squadron of the 45th Infantry Division. He participated with this unit in the campaigns of Poland and France, again earning the Iron Cross First Class. During Operation *Barbarossa*, he was placed in command of mobile units, with which he made deep raids between enemy lines. Promoted to *Oberstleutnant* in August 1941, he was decorated with the Knight's Cross as commander of the *Aukfl.Abt.45*, on September 4, 1941. In September 1941, the *Abteilung Pannwitz* reported new successes and his commander was proposed for award of the Oak Leaves. But after refusing to lead his men on a suicide mission, the proposal was shelved. In November 1941, while fighting under the *6.Armee*, he left his command for health reasons.

From December 1, 1941, he was transferred to the OKH headquarters in Lötzen with the position of expert adviser at the headquarters of the motorized units. On September 20, 1942, Pannwitz obtained authorization to travel to the regions of Don, Kuban and Terek to become acquainted with the 'Cossack' problem. In Maikop, he met with *General der Kavallerie* Ernst-August Köstring[1] and inspected a Cossack regiment. On September 27, he was received by the commander of the 1st Army, *Generaloberst* von Kleist, who encouraged him in his project. On September 28, Pannwitz inspected the *Jungschulz* regiment in Atchikulak.

Oberst **Helmuth von Pannwitz.**

Don Cossacks, 1942.

Upon his arrival, he was greeted by the *Oberstleutnant* von Jungschulz, surrounded by his bodyguard, in the typical Cossack uniform. After spending a few days with these units, he inspected a battalion of Turkmen volunteers in the company of General Köstring.

According to what the author Kern wrote[2]: ".... *The German commander of this battalion, was very rigid in enforcing military discipline, completely forgetting that he was not in command of Berliners. The Turkmens, who at the beginning had enlisted with great enthusiasm, were now almost forced to execute orders.*" After this visit, Pannwitz immediately noted what the difficulties were regarding the integration of foreign volunteers into the Wehrmacht. On his return, he met again once again with von Kleist, to whom he confided his impressions: "... *If the Cossacks are ready to fight Bolshevism, they will do so only if they are guaranteed their freedom*".

On October 1, 1942, Pannwitz became aware of his mission to the OKH General Staff and obtained authorization from Zeitzler to form a large Cossack unit. He then began, not without difficulty, to review all the Cossack units present and on November 8, 1942, he received the title, still very theoretical, of commander in chief of all the Cossack units in the German army with the mission of forming in the shortest time possible a Cossack division. To avoid attracting the attention of party dignitaries and Gauleiters (especially Erich Koch, *Gauleiter* of Ukraine), formally opposed to the recruitment of inferior men, the adjective 'Cossack' was implied and future unity was designated in official documents like *Reiterverband Pannwitz*.

On November 15, Pannwitz left the OKH for the Army General Staff of Group A in Voroshilovsk, where he began to form the organization of his future division and to group a command structure embryo. The critical situation of the front, with the *6.Armee* surrounded in Stalingrad, prevented him from carrying out his mission in an optimal way. Pannwitz was in fact appointed at the head of a tactical group consisting of an armored brigade, a

Romanian cavalry brigade, a Romanian battery, Cossack units taken from Cossack units organized by the hetman Pavlov and the various German formations that had been tasked to ward off the threat on the right flank of *4.Pz.Armee* (Hoth), launched to the rescue of *6.Armee*. At the head of this heterogeneous grouping of about a thousand men, Pannwitz successfully carried out his mission. Thanks to the action of the Cossack cavalrymen who fought like devils, more than three thousand Soviet soldiers were captured and much war booty was recovered: two divisions of Soviet cavalry (61st and 81st) and a Soviet infantry division in the sector of Pimen Tcherni were destroyed and Nébikov.

A German Cossack unit on the Eastern Front, Autumn 1942.

Von Pannwitz and Cossacks horsemen, 1943.

Cited on the agenda of the 4th Romanian army, Oberst von Pannwitz was awarded the Romanian Order of Michael the Brave (3rd class) and, on December 24, 1942, he added the Oak Leaves to his Knight's Cross. On January 6, 1943, Pannwitz, completely impressed by the effectiveness and combativeness of the Cossacks, went again to the OKH to examine with General Zeitzler the problem of the formation of the Cossack units. Then, on January 13, 1943, he was summoned to the headquarters of the *Führer*, to receive from Hitler himself, the Oak Leaves for his Knight's Cross. On the occasion, Hitler encouraged him in his venture to recruit the Cossacks into the German armed forces.

(To be continued)

Notes

[1] An old military representative in Moscow, Köstring, a Russian specialist, having been born in Moscow himself, had been appointed in August 1942, general in charge of the Caucasus.

[2] Erich Kern, "Les Cosaques de Hitler", Paris 1963.

Bibliography

Massimiliano Afiero, "*I volontari stranieri di Hitler*", Ritter edizioni
Francois de Lannoy, "*Les cosacques de Pannwitz*", Editions Heimdal
D. Littlejohn, "*Foreign Legion of the Third Reich, Vol. 4*", R. Bender Publishing
Erich Kern, "*I Cosacchi di Hitler*", Ritter edizioni

The Panzerfaust
by Massimiliano Afiero

German *Luftwaffe* soldier with a *Panzerfaust*.

***Grossdeutschland* division soldier with a *Panzerfaust*.**

The *Panzerfaust*, literally *"armored fist"*, was probably the most famous antitank weapon of the Second World War, and was an expression of German ingenuity. The strong point of this design undoubtedly was having incorporated into a single weapon a high penetration capability, against which no armor of those times was able to withstand, coupled with extreme simplicity of use. Added to those strong points were other characteristics not of secondary importance, such as light weight, portability and a production process that was rather simple and economical which contributed to make the *Panzerfaust* an enviable, versatile and most of all a very effective weapon. The basic idea of the design was, in fact, that of a single-shot weapon with high destructive potential, to be used in brief actions conducted by even just a single soldier, with the aim of inflicting significant damage on the enemy with a minimum expenditure of resources, both in human as well as material terms. These qualities married up well with *Blitzkrieg* tactics, based on the joint action of infantry and armored vehicles, but in 1939 the weapon was still a far-off dream and was not able to reach the front until summer of 1943. Despite that, the *Panzerfaust* proved to be an irreplaceable weapon, widely used by German *Panzergrenadiere* with excellent results, and soon became a nightmare for enemy tank crews.

Even during the final days of the war, in spite of the fact that the fate of the war was by now sealed, the *Panzerfaust* was among the main players in the battle for Berlin, thanks to the tenacity of young members of the *Hitlerjugend* and of the French volunteers of the *33.Waffen-Gren.Division der SS Charlemagne*, who demonstrated their courage in attacks against Soviet tanks in the vain attempt to defend the city which was already occupied.

Left, a group of German soldiers armed with *Panzerfaust* anti-tank weapons, next to a knocked-out Soviet *T-34*, Latvia, 1944. Right photo, German paratroopers guarding the entrance to the Castel Sant'Angelo in Rome. *MG-42* and a *Panzerfaust* are ready for use.

A German Panzerknacker, decorated with three tank destruction badge, with a *Panzerfaust*.

A new antitank concept

During the winter of 1941, the Germans realized that development of traditional antitank weapons would not be able to guarantee results suitable to deal with increasingly better protected and faster armored vehicles. In essence, even if the Germans had focused all of their efforts on development of rifles and guns, the increase in performance would have soon reached a *"physiological"* limit, tied to the mechanical characteristics of those weapons, beyond which any further effort would have not led to any improvement. In addition to increasing the caliber, to the detriment of the size and weight of the weapon, or replacement of traditional ammunition with higher-performance rounds, they would have led to an ever decreasing improvement of performance tending towards zero. In order to cope effectively with enemy tanks, especially the Soviet *JS-I (Josef Stalin I)* and *JS-II*, a radical, ground-breaking solution was needed, of necessity divorced from the mechanical limits of traditional weapons and from the idea that penetrating ability depended, in large measure, on the kinetic velocity of the projectile and on its caliber. These were the reasons why German talent was pushed to carry out research in other directions and to follow new avenues, devoting less and less time and resources to the development of traditional antitank weapons, whose production, beginning in 1943, became daily increasingly difficult because of the lack of raw materials.

T-34 knocked out too late to prevent it from running over a *Pak 36* anti-tank gun.

A *Pak 36* fitted with a *Stielgranate 41.*

An anti-tank gun with a *Stielgranate 41* in action.

In particular, it was Doctor Heinrich Langweiler of the *Hugo Schneider Aktien Gesellschaf* of Leipzig who focused attention on development of a weapon that was completely divorced from the logic of the rifle and cannon, in favor of a design that was innovative and revolutionary from the point of view of both performance as well as of the production process. German scientists had for some time begun to take the first steps towards new solutions with the intent to improve the performance of weapons already at the front. In particular, the introduction of the *Stielgranate 41* enabled the traditional *Pak* to significantly increase their performance to face off against the Soviet *T-34* tank. What made these munitions particularly effective was the use of the "shaped charge" principle instead of the traditional metal projectile. Thanks to this system, the Germans realized that this type of munition was an effective answer to their unceasing need to face the challenge posed by enemy tanks, especially on the Eastern Front where the Soviets, in 1942, began to field an increasingly greater number of armored forces. In the wake of studies conducted for development of the *Sturmgewehr 41*, Doctor Langweiler, by request of the German general staff, began to work on the design of the *Panzerfaust* in 1941.

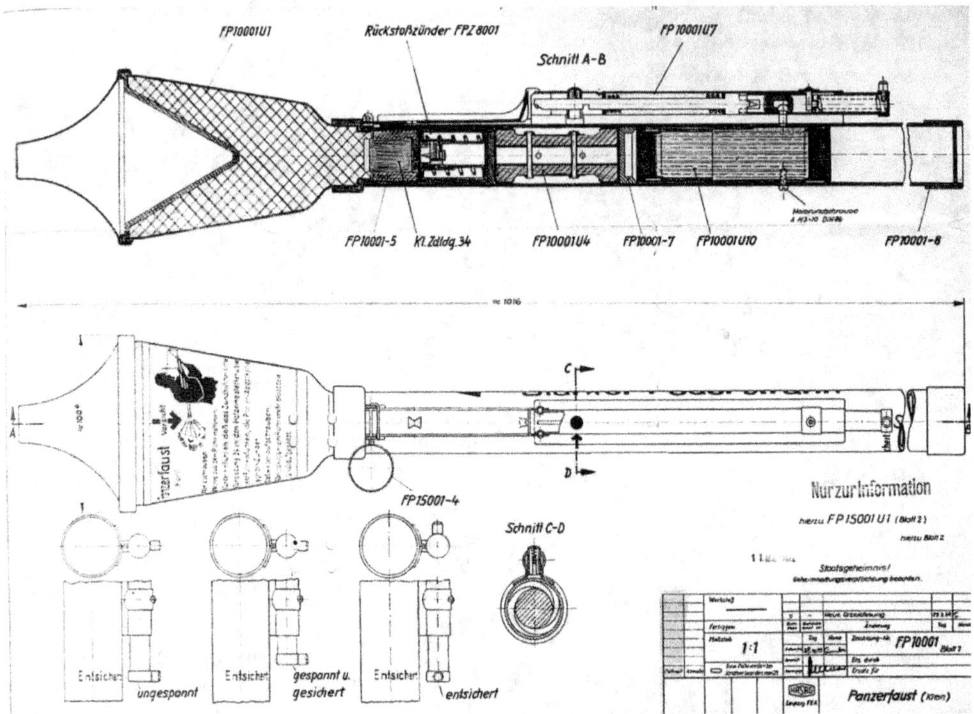

Cutaway of the *Faustpatrone Klein*, from original period documentation; clearly visible is the simple firing mechanism activated by the metal lever on the launch tube.

A *Luftwaffe* soldier with a *Faustpatrone Klein*.

The first fruit of his work was the *Faustpatrone Klein*, which was produced by *HASAG Hugo Schneider AG* of Leipzig. Langweiler and his team of engineers came up with a very simple weapon, made up of two main parts: a launch tube, fitted with a simple trigger, and a projectile of oversize proportions and of unusual shape. The projectile, called the *Faustpatrone*, was the real heart of the weapon. Capitalizing upon the physical phenomenon of the so-called "shaped charge", compared to the normal 13.2x92mm *Mauser* antitank rounds or the grenades of the *Granatbüchse 39*, it acted against armor by melting it, thanks to an impact force of ten million kilograms per square centimeter that it was able to develop. Although the earliest experiments gave encouraging results in terms of performance as well as of practicality of use, the weapon displayed some serious shortcomings. A rudimentary sighting system was lacking but most of all the design of the *Faustpatrone* was imperfect in that, unless the shot was flawless, the projectile, instead of melting the armor plate, would bounce off it.

A grenadier from the *12.SS-Panzer-Division 'Hitlerjugend'* with a *Faustpatrone* in Normandy, near a destroyed *Sherman* tank, Summer 1944.

A *Luftwaffe* soldier during firing tests with the Faustpatrone Klein.

German police personnel in Italy armed with the *Panzerfaust Klein*.

For those reasons the *Fauspatrone Klein* had a brief life and was soon replaced by an updated version, the *Panzerfaust 30*, with the "30" indicating the maximum range of the weapon, expressed in meters. The first employment of the *Panzerfaust 30* at the front, in August 1943, was encouraging, even though field experience soon revealed another shortcoming: the range. The declared 30 meters, which in the frenzy of combat could decline considerably, were insufficient to avert the danger of the soldier being killed while approaching close to the target or, after having fired, while moving away from it. Because of this, the HASAG engineers, led by Doctor Langweiler, pushed the weapon's performance by increasing the propellant charge from 95 grams to 134 grams, guaranteeing a velocity of 45 m/sec and a range of sixty meters: thus was born the *Panzerfaust 60*, the most widely used version during the Second World War. The *Panzerfaust 60* was followed by the

Panzerfaust 100 in November 1944, whose performance, with a range of a hundred meters and a projectile velocity of 60 m/sec, were upgraded without altering the design or structure of the weapon, thanks to a two-stage propellant that imparted greater thrust to the projectile. Despite the fact that the war was by now compromised, the evolution of the *Panzerfaust* did not encounter any obstacles; in fact, beginning in January 1945, development of the *Panzerfaust 150* began, followed by a brief appearance in the field in March with issue of a small number to the troops engaged in the exhausting combat.

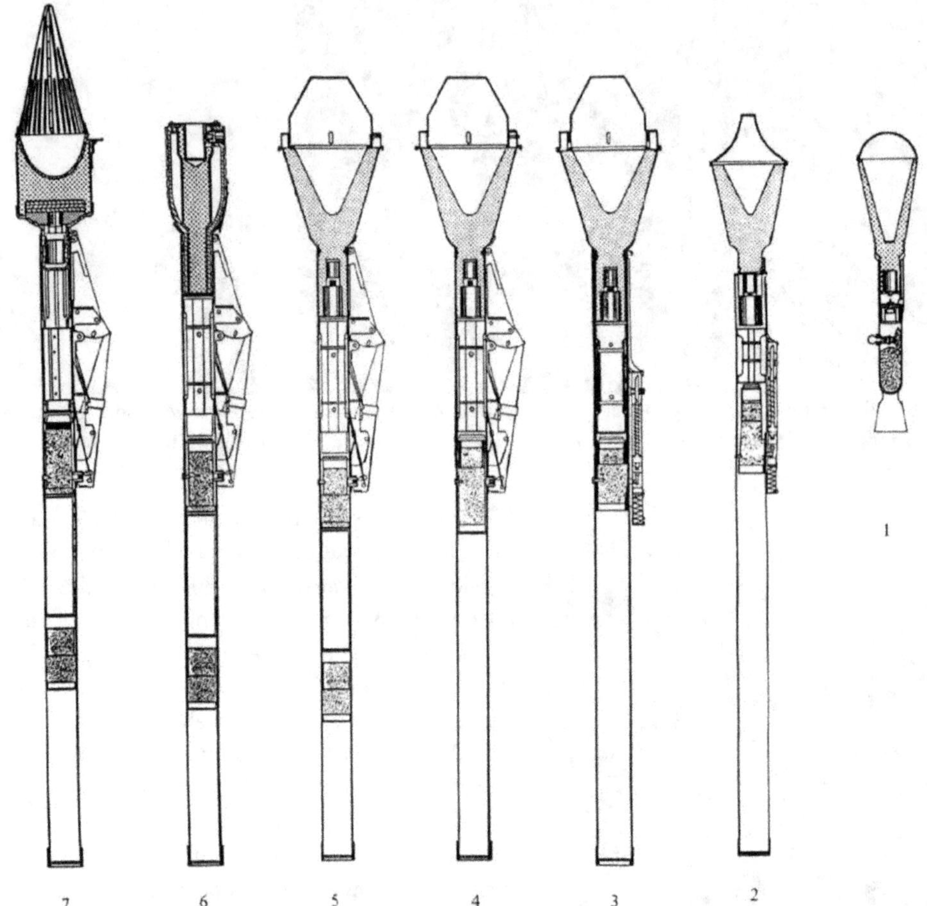

1: *Faustpatrone*, 2: *Panzerfaust Klein*, 3: *Panzerfaust Gross*, 4: *Panzerfaust 60 m*, 5: *Panzerfaust 100 m*, 6: *Splitterfaust*, 7: *Panzerfaust 150 m.*

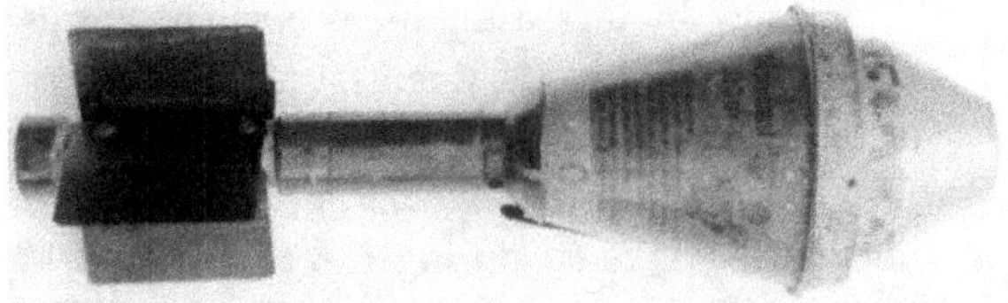

The two-stage projectile of the *Panzerfaust 100*.

The *Panzerfaust 150* represented the turning point in the history of this weapon, as it introduced the ability to use the launch tube up to ten times, while in earlier versions the launch tube, once used, was discarded. But the new features did not end there: in addition to the increased performance (150 meter range, 85 m/sec projectile velocity) a new design of the warhead was introduced which enabled the distance at which the explosion of the shaped charge occurred to be controlled with greater accuracy, in order to guarantee maximum destructive effect. The *Panzerfaust 150* was to have been followed by the *Panzerfaust 250*, but that design remained on paper even though its production had been planned by the Germans for September 1945.

Ukraine 1944: a German soldier showing the correct firing position with a *Panzerfaust 30*, during an exercise.

A German soldier armed with a *Panzerfaust 150*.

How the weapon functions

All of the versions produced, beyond the differences in performance, based their functioning on the same principle: that of the "shaped charge". Thanks to this system, which had been known since the time of the discovery of gunpowder and applied to ballistic science in 1888 by the American engineer Charles E. Munroe, it is possible to achieve a high destructive capability by employing a small quantity of explosive. The explosive has to be arranged so that on the inside of a conical of semi-spherical charge the heat produced by the explosion is concentrated onto a single point in order to obtain a plasma jet at high temperature and with a significant impact force, able to penetrate, by melting, any type of steel.

Eastern front: *Waffen-SS* soldiers, sheltering in a trench, with a *Panzerfaust 60.*

A formidable weapon, enough to earn a place on the cover of period magazine.

A German NCO preparing a *Panzerfaust 60* for firing, during an exercise for tank hunter students...

Thus conceived, the 2.9 kg warhead of the *Panzerfaust*, exploding, generated gases which hit the target at 8,000 m/sec with a force of ten million kilograms per square centimeter, regardless of its kinetic energy; in fact, with respect to armor penetration, the kinetic velocity of the projectile was irrelevant as the impact force was generated by the shaped charge in the warhead (giving it its characteristic large head). However, to achieve a similar effect, it was necessary that the charge explode at the right moment, in other words, not too soon and not too late, with respect to the impact against the target; in the first instance, in fact, the effect generated by the plasma would be dispersed into the air and would not cause significant damage to the tank; in the second instance, to the contrary, the explosion against the target would not give the gases exploding inside the projectile to reach a high enough temperature to enable the armor to be penetrated.

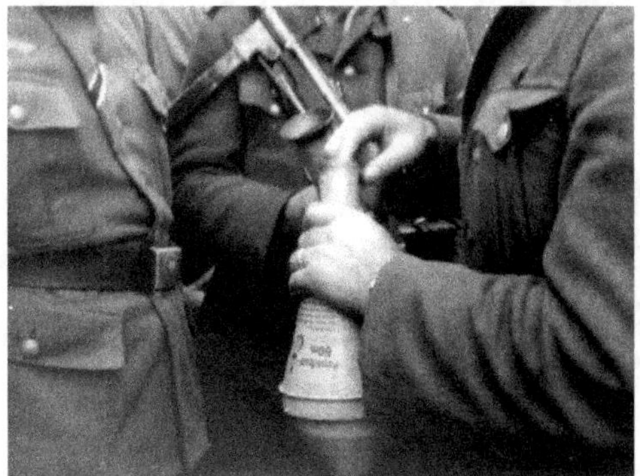

...calculating distance and ready to fire.

A *Panzerknacker* observing a knocked-out tank.

A soldier armed with a *Panzerfaust* ready to fire.

In addition, in order to guarantee a powerful explosion, it was necessary to avoid having the projectile rotating on its own axis while in flight towards the target (such as happens normally for small arms ammunition); to that end the rocket was fitted with small stabilizer fins in the rear portion, which opened after leaving the launch tube. The presence of the stabilizer fins worked to the detriment of the projectile's velocity and against its accuracy, but on the other hand, as the *Panzerfaust* was conceived for short-range engagements, those factors could be considered secondary to the destructive effect that was sought. With respect to the single use launch tube, which we can consider to be a sort of large cartridge containing the projectile, it was used to ignite the launch charge located in the terminal portion of the projectile by means of a primer, as is the case in common light arms.

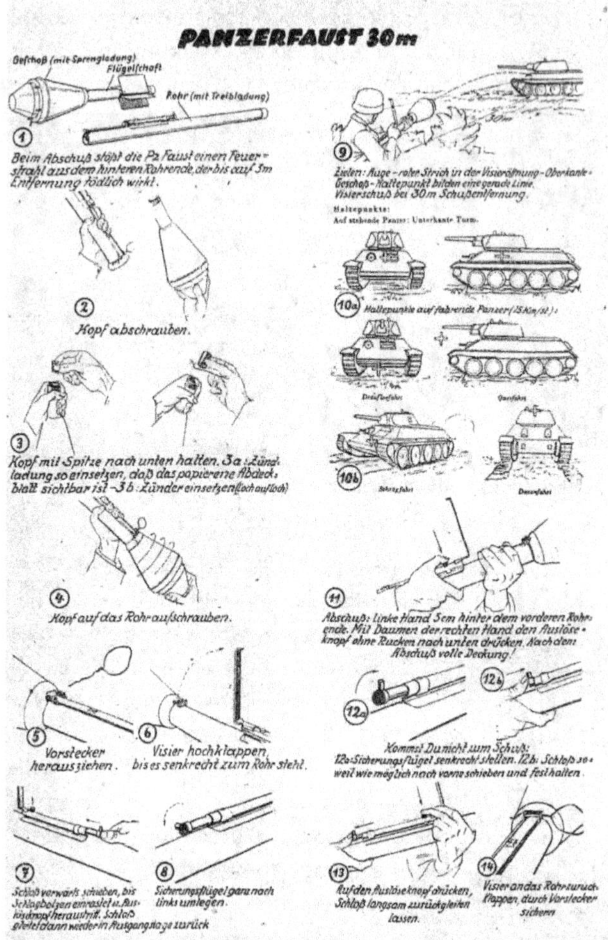

Manual for the *Panzerfaust 30*, with all instructions for its use and preparation for firing against tanks.

A German soldier armed with a *Panzerfaust*.

The gases exploding inside the tube were expelled through the rear and the jet that was produced could be very dangerous for both the operator as well as other soldiers. Not by accident, each weapon bore a label showing the minimum safe distance (to the rear), free of all obstacles, for which it was possible to fire: ten meters. The launch tube was also fitted with a sort of sight with vertical holes which, like a rear sight, helped the operator to calculate to a fairly approximate degree the distance to the target and to assess the best position from which to fire. The *Panzerfaust*, as can be easily perceived, was a very simple weapon to produce and to use; its very simplicity, which meant that it could be used by any soldier, was probably one of its biggest shortcomings from the standpoint of "human costs". In fact, it was often used with a certain degree of inattention or superficial care by those who were least skilled, despite the warning printed in large red letters on the launch tube *"Achtung! Feuerstrahl!"* (*Attention! Fire Spurt!*), accidents caused by the weapon's back-blast were not uncommon.

Bibliography

M. Afiero, "*SS-Panzerknacker:uomini contro carri*", Soldiershop Publishing

M. Afiero, "*Panzerknacker*", Kagero Publishing

WW2 AXIS
FORCES

SOLDIERSHOP
PUBLISHING
BOOKS TO COLLECT

SOLDIERSHOP
PUBLISHING
BOOKS TO COLLECT